CLASSIC ROCK CLIMBS
NUMBER 23

T0346543

LYONS AREA
COLORADO

by
Peter Hubbel

CHOCKSTONE

FALCON®

HELENA, MONTANA

AFALCONGUIDE®

Falcon® Publishing is continually expanding its list of recreation guidebooks. All books include detailed descriptions, accurate maps, and all the information necessary for enjoyable trips. You can order extra copies of this book and get information and prices for other Falcon® guidebooks by writing Falcon, P.O. Box 1718, Helena, MT 59624 or calling toll free 1-800-582-2665. Also, please ask for a free copy of our current catalog. Visit our website at www.falconguide.com

©1999 Peter Hubbel
Printed in the United States of America

1 2 3 4 5 6 7 8 9 0 MG 04 03 02 01 00 99

ISBN 1-57540-025-1 *Classic Rock Climbs* series
    1-57540-048-0 *Classic Rock Climbs 23: Lyons Area, Colorado*

Falcon, FalconGuide, and Chockstone are registered trademarks of Falcon® Publishing, Inc.

All rights reserved, including the right to reproduce this book or parts thereof in any form, except for inclusion of brief quotations in a review.

All black-and-white photos by the author unless noted otherwise.
Cover photo by Ruel Chapman.

Cataloging information on file with the Library of Congress.

CAUTION

Outdoor recreational activities are by their very nature potentially hazardous. All participants in such activities must assume the responsibility for their own actions and safety. The information contained in this guidebook cannot replace sound judgment and good decision-making skills, which help reduce risk exposure, nor does the scope of this book allow for disclosure of all the potential hazards and risks involved in such activities.

Learn as much as possible about the outdoor recreational activities in which you participate, prepare for the unexpected, and be cautious. The reward will be a safer and more enjoyable experience.

 Text pages printed on recycled paper

WARNING:
CLIMBING IS A SPORT WHERE
YOU MAY BE SERIOUSLY INJURED OR DIE.
READ THIS BEFORE YOU USE THIS BOOK.

This guidebook is a compilation of unverified information gathered from many different climbers. The author cannot assure the accuracy of any of the information in this book, including the topos and route descriptions, the difficulty ratings, and the protection ratings. These may be incorrect or misleading and it is impossible for any one author to climb all the routes to confirm the information about each route. Also, ratings of climbing difficulty and danger are always subjective and depend on the physical characteristics (for example, height), experience, technical ability, confidence and physical fitness of the climber who supplied the rating. Additionally, climbers who achieve first ascents sometimes underrate the difficulty or danger of the climbing route out of fear of being ridiculed if a climb is later down-rated by subsequent ascents. Therefore, be warned that you must exercise your own judgment on where a climbing route goes, its difficulty and your ability to safely protect yourself from the risks of rock climbing. Examples of some of these risks are: falling due to technical difficulty or due to natural hazards such as holds breaking, falling rock, climbing equipment dropped by other climbers, hazards of weather and lightning, your own equipment failure, and failure or absence of fixed protection.

You should not depend on any information gleaned from this book for your personal safety; your safety depends on your own good judgment, based on experience and a realistic assessment of your climbing ability. If you have any doubt as to your ability to safely climb a route described in this book, do not attempt it.

The following are some ways to make your use of this book safer:

1. Consultation: You should consult with other climbers about the difficulty and danger of a particular climb prior to attempting it. Most local climbers are glad to give advice on routes in their area and we suggest that you contact locals to confirm ratings and safety of particular routes and to obtain first-hand information about a route chosen from this book.

2. Instruction: Most climbing areas have local climbing instructors and guides available. We recommend that you engage an instructor or guide to learn safety techniques and to become familiar with the routes and hazards of the areas described in this book. Even after you are proficient in climbing safely, occasional use of a guide is a safe way to raise your climbing standard and learn advanced techniques.

3. Fixed Protection: Many of the routes in this book use bolts and pitons which are permanently placed in the rock. Because of variances in the manner of placement, weathering, metal fatigue, the quality of the metal used, and many other factors, these fixed protection pieces should always be considered suspect and should always be backed up by equipment that you place yourself. Never depend for your safety on a single piece of fixed protection because you never can tell whether it will hold weight, and in some cases, fixed protection may have been removed or is now absent.

Be aware of the following specific potential hazards which could arise in using this book:

1. Misdescriptions of Routes: If you climb a route and you have a doubt as to where the route may go, you should not go on unless you are sure that you can go that way safely. Route descriptions and topos in this book may be inaccurate or misleading.

2. Incorrect Difficulty Rating: A route may, in fact, be more difficult than the rating indicates. Do not be lulled into a false sense of security by the difficulty rating.

3. Incorrect Protection Rating: If you climb a route and you are unable to arrange adequate protection from the risk of falling through the use of fixed pitons or bolts and by placing your own protection devices, do not assume that there is adequate protection available higher just because the route protection rating indicates the route is not an "X" or an "R" rating. Every route is potentially an "X" (a fall may be deadly), due to the inherent hazards of climbing – including, for example, failure or absence of fixed protection, your own equipment's failure, or improper use of climbing equipment.

THERE ARE NO WARRANTIES, WHETHER EXPRESS OR IMPLIED, THAT THIS GUIDEBOOK IS ACCURATE OR THAT THE INFORMATION CONTAINED IN IT IS RELIABLE. THERE ARE NO WARRANTIES OF FITNESS FOR A PARTICULAR PURPOSE OR THAT THIS GUIDE IS MERCHANTABLE. YOUR USE OF THIS BOOK INDICATES YOUR ASSUMPTION OF THE RISK THAT IT MAY CONTAIN ERRORS AND IS AN ACKNOWLEDGMENT OF YOUR OWN SOLE RESPONSIBILITY FOR YOUR CLIMBING SAFETY.

This book is dedicated with love to Mary Katherine Norman.

ACKNOWLEDGMENTS

As with all guidebooks, a great many people end up contributing information in one form or another. The author wishes to thank the following people: Alvino Pon, Mark Rolofson, Jeffery Butterfield, Ruell Chapman, Peter Donelan, Deaun Schovajsa, CT Traufield, Chris King, Harry Kent, Steve Komito, Alan Mosiman, Dave Rice, Steve Hong, Ben Colkitt & Natalie Frei, Gene Ellis, Hector Galbraith.

Special thanks goes to the following people: Deaun Schovajsa for the intro and proofreading; CT Traufield for general moral support, proof reading, and sense of adventure; Ben Colkitt and Natalie Frei for continuing hospitality and computer education; Mary Katherine Norman for moral support and proofreading; Jeffery Butterfield and Ruell Chapman for photos; Tom Brown, Gene Ellis, Alvino Pon, and Mark Rolofson for route info; Michael Cutter for photos; Jay Kinghorn for photos and route information.

ALVINO PON ON UPSIDE THE CRANIUM. MONKEY SKULL. PHOTO BY RUEL CHAPMAN.

TABLE OF CONTENTS

INTRODUCTION	**1**
GETTING THERE	2
ACCESS ISSUES	2
NEARBY CLIMBING	2
CAMPING AND NEARBY AMENITIES	2
AREA ROAD MAP	3
BUTTONROCK DAM	**4**
OVERVIEW MAP	4
DIRECTIONS	5
CAMPING AND RECREATION	6
ENTRYWAY SLABS	8
BUICK ROCKS	8
HITLER'S SEX LIFE	9
ROB'S ROCK	11
AQUEDUCT ROCK	12
OLD YELLAR FORMATION	13
RIVER WALL	13
TIGERS IN LIPSTICK FORMATION	18
THE BULLET	19
BOULDERING WALL	20
SOUTH ST. VRAIN	**21**
GPS LOCATIONS AND MILEAGE	22
LOCATOR MAP	23
SCOUT ROCK	24
GUARDIAN ROCK	25
MUSHROOM MASSIF	26
DESDOMONA	28

DECEMBER WALL	29
THE SENTINEL	30
ROADSIDE ROCK	31
SWEAT LOAF	32
SUPERCHUNK	33
INFIRMARY SLAB AREA AND NARROWS OVERVIEW MAP	34
LOWER INFIRMARY SLABS	35
UPPER INFIRMARY SLABS	36
CLINICAL PINNACLE	36
LEFT INFIRMARY SLABS	37
OBSERVATORY ROCK	38
YE OLDE ROCK	40
NORTH NARROW SLABS	41
SOUTH NARROW SLABS	42
VRAIN DEAD FORMATION	43
SPIRE ROCK	45
BULLSHIT ROCK	46
WAILING WALL	47
LITTLE OGRE	48
MONKEY SKULL	50
TROJAN BUNNY BUTTRESS	52
LEATHERFACE	53
ACROPHILE ROCK	54
HIDEAWAY DOME	55
THE FANG	56
VIOLATOR BUTTRESS	57
THE WATCHTOWER	58
PIZ BADILLE	61
OLD STAGE WALL	63
GOLDEN GATE CANYON	**64**
OVERVIEW MAP	64
DIRECTIONS	66
CAMPING AND RECREATION	66
GOLDEN GATE DETAIL MAP	67
SON OF RALSTON	68
RALSTON ROOST	69
MOUNT THORIDIN	71
RAVEN KNOB	73
THORODIN SLAB	74
GROSS RESERVOIR AREA	**76**
OVERVIEW MAP	76
ZEBRA ROCK AND PINECLIFFE	77
CAMPING AND RECREATION	77
INDEXES	**81**
INDEX BY GRADE	81
INDEX BY ROUTE NAME	84

BEAUTIFUL SCENERY NEAR BUTTONROCK.

LYONS AREA

By Deaun Schovajsa

The eastern slope of Colorado's Rocky Mountains, and the foothills, mesas, canyons and plains that collide along their eastern edge, make up what is collectively called the Front Range. With literally dozens of unique, individual climbing destinations, the Front Range offers an abundance and variety of rock climbing that is perhaps unmatched in any other state. This guide, along with companion "classic" guides from Falcon/Chockstone, will provide up-to-date beta on the diverse, rapidly developing Front Range region. Current route information, maps, topos and access news help you get where you want to go.

The canyons formed by the North and South Forks of the St. Vrain River make up the Lyons Area. Visited for many years by locals and a few select Denver-Boulder residents, the area has been "rediscovered" in recent years. New bolted faces, aretes, overhanging walls and hard thin cracks combine with an excellent selection of easy to moderate crack routes to create a playground enjoyable to both the seasoned veteran and novice alike.

The river canyons are beautiful recreation areas popular with hikers and fishermen as well as climbers. Granite domes, shaped originally by glaciers, then by rain, wind, snow, and ice, dot the upper slopes of South St. Vrain. Steep walls carved by the swift, icy runoff over millions of years line the lower portions of the canyons. A variety of hearty pines, aspens and cottonwood trees manage to thrive in the rocky terrain. Golden eagles and red-tailed hawks soar overhead, hunting and fishing the river bottoms below. Despite easy road access along the rivers, the area remains remarkably pristine. Only a few primitive trails exist for hiking, and some thread their way to popular crags.

GETTING THERE   The South St. Vrain Canyon and North St. Vrain/Buttonrock Dam Areas are very near to the town of Lyons, Colorado. Lyons is about twenty minutes north of Boulder on Hwy. 36. From the Junction of hwy 36 and 7 turn left (south) on Hwy 7 for the South St. Vrain Canyon area. For the North St. Vrain/Buttonrock Dam Area continue just past Lyons on Hwy 36 to county road 80 where you will go south. Refer to the individual chapter intros for complete directions and road maps of the respective areas.

ACCESS ISSUES   Currently no access problems exist for this area. However, as climbing becomes more popular, our need to minimize our impact in all of the areas we visit becomes greater. The North St. Vrain River is run by the City of Longmont as a drinking water supply, so no swimming or inner-tubing is allowed. No camping.

NEARBY CLIMBING   In the Estes Park area, Lumpy Ridge and Rocky Mountain National Park provide excellent rock climbing during the warmer months. Of course, Boulder Canyon, Eldorado Canyon, and the Flatirons are all within minutes of the Boulder area. Just south of Boulder, the city of Golden yields Golden Cliffs and Clear Creek Canyon, two relatively new sport climbing areas.

CAMPING AND NEARBY AMENITIES   Public camping is available in Rocky Mountain National Park. Limited camping is available in the South St. Vrain Canyon. Motel and hotel accommodations are available in Estes Park or Boulder. Some dining can be found in Lyons, along with service stations. Boulder has a great selection of all services including restaurants, bars, movie theaters, night clubs, climbing shops, and several climbing gyms.

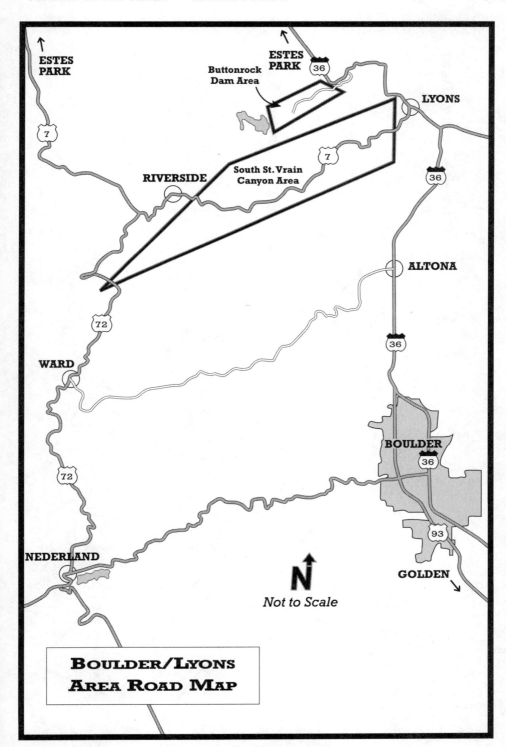

ESTES
PARK

ESTES
PARK

Buttonrock
Dam Area

LYONS

7

South St. Vrain
Canyon Area

7

RIVERSIDE

36

ALTONA

72

36

WARD

72

BOULDER

36

NEDERLAND

93

N
Not to Scale

GOLDEN

**BOULDER/LYONS
AREA ROAD MAP**

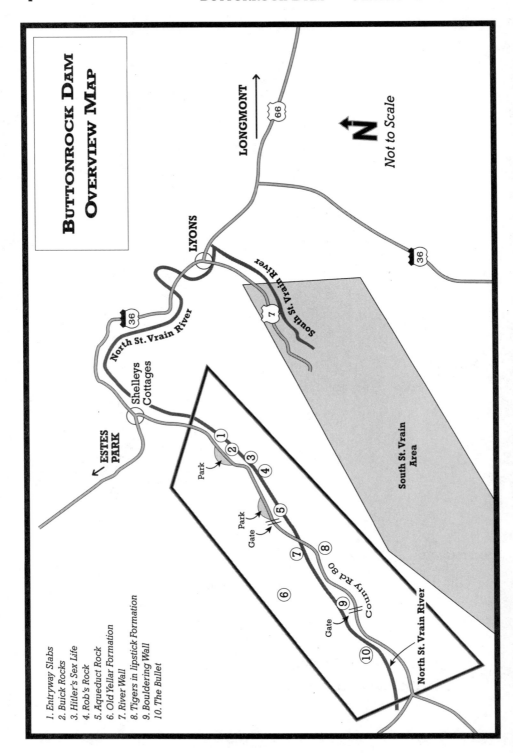

BUTTONROCK DAM OVERVIEW MAP

Not to Scale

N

LONGMONT

LYONS

ESTES PARK

Shelleys Cottages

North St. Vrain River

South St. Vrain River

South St. Vrain Area

North St. Vrain River

County Rd 80

Park

Park
Gate

Gate

1. Entryway Slabs
2. Buick Rocks
3. Hitler's Sex Life
4. Rob's Rock
5. Aqueduct Rock
6. Old Yellar Formation
7. River Wall
8. Tigers in lipstick Formation
9. Bouldering Wall
10. The Bullet

BUTTONROCK DAM AREA

"Would you tell me, please, which way I ought to go from here?"
"That depends a good deal on where you want to get to," said the Cat.
"I don't much care where —," said Alice.
"Then it doesn't matter which way you go," said the Cat.
"— so long as I get somewhere," Alice added as an explanation.
"Oh, you're sure to do that," said the Cat, "if you only walk long enough"

Lewis Carroll
Alice in Wonderland

Buttonrock Dam area offers some of the most concentrated grouping of hard rock climbs in this guidebook as well as more moderate routes. With the exception of the Old Yellar Formation and The Bullet, most climbs are within a 5-minute walk from your car.

The Buttonrock Dam area follows the North St. Vrain River and the climbing is on granite. The climbs at the beginning of the canyon are primarily crack climbs. The climbing farther up the canyon, with some exceptions, consists of hard face climbs.

DIRECTIONS To get there, go right at the junction of Highways 36 and 7 [GPS 0476883/4452693] heading towards Estes Park. After about 3.7 miles, turn left at the Shelly's Cottages sign (County Road 80)[GPS 0473285/4454781]. One-half mile after the turn are the Entryway Slabs on the left. Around the corner, .1 mile farther, are Buick Rocks and Hitler's Sex Life [GPS 0472721/4454157], also on the left.

Located .1 mile past this formation and about 300' above the road, again on the left, is Rob's Rock.[GPS 0472865/4454048] Continuing past Hitler's Sex Life for another 2.3 miles brings you to a steel gate and parking. Aqueduct Rock is on your left before crossing through the gate. River Wall [GPS0470606/4453198] is the formation immediately past the gate on the right.

The best approach for River Wall and the the Old Yellar Formation, (especially during times of high water) starts on the right, just before you cross the gate. Use the rappel bolts at the top of The Box to access River Wall. Continue up the trail above River Wall as it diagonals uphill to reach the Old Yellar Formation.

Three hundred feet past River Wall on the left, just off the road, is the small Tigers In Lipstick Formation.[GPS 0470388/4453168]. Two miles or so further past the second gate and about 60 yards uphill is The Bullet, [GPS 0469460/4452351]where all but two of the climbs are crack climbs. Between The Bullet and River Wall is the Bouldering Wall [GPS 0469712/4452449] also on the right.

Duncan Ferquson, Paul Piana, George Brackseick and Susanne Jackson as well as other climbers, were responsible for some of the first routes on Buick Rocks and Hitler's Sex Life. Mark Wilford and Steve Mammen put up routes such as Tick Alert and Local Motion as well as routes on the River Wall and The Bullet. Most of the climbs on River Wall were done in the late '80s by a virtual who's who of Boulder climbers as well as visiting Paul Piana: Bob Horan, Rob Candeleria, Colin Lantz, Beth Wald, Harold Quib, Wolfgang Schweiger, Chip Ruckgraber, Jeff Gruenberg and the late Katherine Frier.

Pat Adams was involved lately in one of the newer additions right of New Horizons; Brother from Another Planet. Steve Hong has been very active on the Old Yellar Formation. Rob Candelaria, in 1993, was responsible for freeing one of the hardest crack climbs in the world on the river wall. This climb, named *Lost Horizons*, was protected by natural gear on lead and rated 5.14a. As of this printing, it hasn't seen a second ascent.

CAMPING AND RECREATION   There is no camping or mountain biking at Buttonrock, but there is some excellent fishing in the North St. Vrain as well as some great hiking trails. Please keep the area as clean as it usually is. The only trashed out spots are the parking areas beneath Entryway Slabs, Buick Rocks and Hitler's Sex Life areas.

ALVINO PON CLIMBING *REUSABLE LOVE BAG* 5.9+ ★★ ON THE PIZ BADILLE. PHOTO BY RUEL CHAPMAN.

1. ENTRYWAY SLABS

1. *Rock Biter* (3) *No pro.*
2. *First Door* (6) *Pro: To 3".*
3. *Joy* (7) *Pro: To 5".*

2. BUICK ROCKS
(FIRST BUTTRESS)

4. *Green Slab* (9+/10a) ★★ *Pro: Misc to 2".*

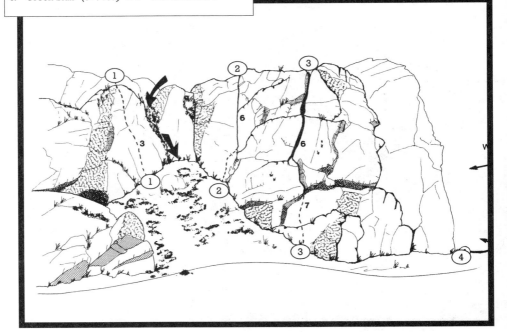

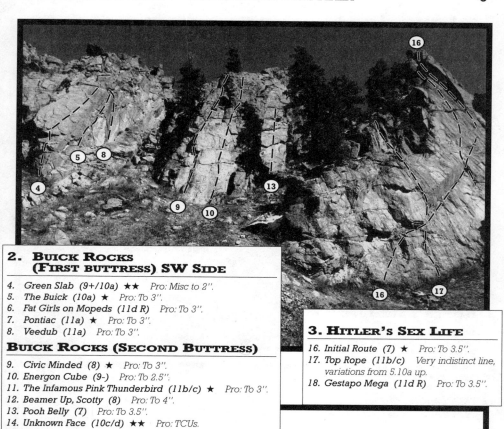

2. BUICK ROCKS (FIRST BUTTRESS) SW SIDE

4. *Green Slab (9+/10a)* ★★   *Pro: Misc to 2''.*
5. *The Buick (10a)* ★   *Pro: To 3''.*
6. *Fat Girls on Mopeds (11d R)*   *Pro: To 3''.*
7. *Pontiac (11a)* ★   *Pro: To 3''.*
8. *Veedub (11a)*   *Pro: To 3''.*

BUICK ROCKS (SECOND BUTTRESS)

9. *Civic Minded (8)* ★   *Pro: To 3''.*
10. *Energon Cube (9-)*   *Pro: To 2.5''.*
11. *The Infamous Pink Thunderbird (11b/c)* ★   *Pro: To 3''.*
12. *Beamer Up, Scotty (8)*   *Pro: To 4''.*
13. *Pooh Belly (7)*   *Pro: To 3.5''.*
14. *Unknown Face (10c/d)* ★★   *Pro: TCUs.*
15. *Kiss Face (10a)*   *Pro: To 2.5''.*

3. HITLER'S SEX LIFE

16. *Initial Route (7)* ★   *Pro: To 3.5''.*
17. *Top Rope (11b/c)*   *Very indistinct line, variations from 5.10a up.*
18. *Gestapo Mega (11d R)*   *Pro: To 3.5''.*

3. HITLER'S SEX LIFE

16. *Initial Route (7)* ★   *Pro: To 3.5''.*
17. *Top Rope (11b/c)*   *Very indistinct line,*
    variations from 5.10a up.
18. *Gestapo Mega (11d R)*   *Pro: To 3.5''.*
19. *Hitler's Sex Life (11c)*   *Pro: To 2''.*

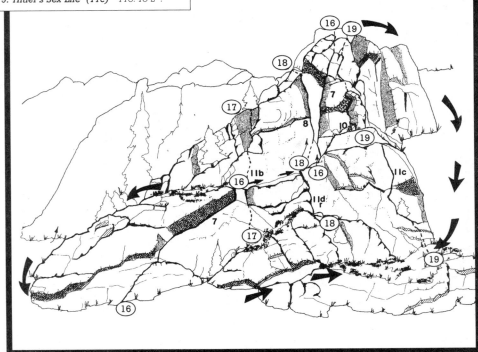

4. Rob's Rock

20. Tain't No Crack (10c) ★★   *Pro: Misc to 3". Free standing rock on left, follows seam with 3 bolts.*

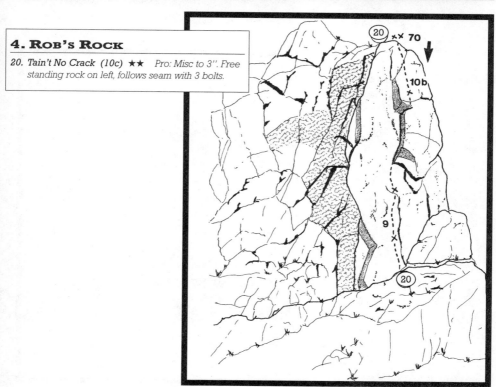

5. AQUEDUCT ROCK

1. *The Pipeline (12a R)*   Pro: To 3/4".

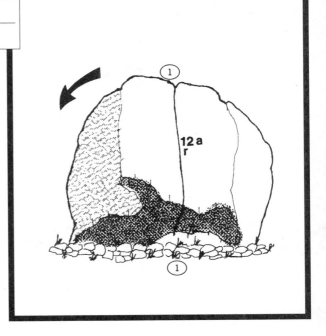

Old Yellar Formation

River Wall

The best approach for River Wall and Old Yellar Formation: Follow trail on right side of parking before gate. There are two bolts on top of The Box to get to the base of River Wall. For Old Yellar, keep high on trail as it traverses the slope, staying quite a bit above River Wall and angling up to Old Yellar.

6. OLD YELLAR FORMATION

4. Old Yellar (13a) ★★★

7. RIVER WALL

15. Red Neck Hero (12a R) ★★★★
23. Shades of Murky Depths (10d)   Pro: To 2.5''.

6. OLD YELLAR FORMATION

1. *Nuttin' but Button (12c)* ★★★
2. *Bambi (12d)* ★★★
3. *Project*
4. *Old Yellar (13a)* ★★★
5. *Project*

6. **Open to Suggestions (11d)**   *No topo.*
    Thirtyfive-foot face on hill above New
    Horizon. Follows seam. Pro: To 3/4".

The following two routes are located near the
Old Yellar Formation, but not on it.

7. **Mercy Slab (10c/d)**   *No topo. Located*
    below and to the right of the Old Yellar
    Formation. Climb a 30 foot face to a right
    leaning corner. Pro: To 2.5".
8. **The Stressor (11c/d)**   *No topo. Takes the*
    thin seam left of Mercy Slab. Pro: To 1.5".

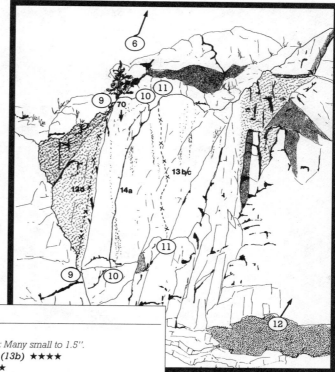

7. RIVER WALL

9. New Horizon (12d) ★★★★
10. Lost Horizon (14a) ★★   Pro: Many small to 1.5''.
11. Brother From Another Planet (13b) ★★★★
12. Big, Big Gunky Man (12a R) ★
13. Pocket Hercules (11d) ★★★   Pro: #5 RP to 2.5'', include 3 1.5''.
14. Big, Big Monkey Man (12b) ★★★   Pro: #5 RP to double 1.5''.
15. Red Neck Hero (12a R) ★★★★

7. RIVER WALL

11. *Brother From Another Planet (13b)* ★★★★
12. *Big, Big Gunky Man (12a R)* ★
13. *Pocket Hercules (11d)* ★★★ Pro: #5 RP To 2.5", include 3 1.5".
14. *Big, Big Monkey Man (12b)* ★★★ Pro: #5 RP to double 1.5".
15. *Red Neck Hero (12a R)* ★★★
16. *Escape From Alcatraz (11b/c)* ★★★
17. *Live Wire (10d)* ★★ Pro: To 2".
18. *Introducing Meteor Dad (10d)* ★★★
19. *The Box (7)* Pro: To 3".
20. *Le Diamant E'ternal (The Eternal Diamond) (13a/b)* ★★★★
21. *Direct (11c/d R)*
22. *Neurosurgeon (12a)* ★★★ Pro: To 2.5".
23. *Shades of Murky Depths (10d)* Pro: To 2.5".
24. *Dihedral (8)* Pro: To 4".
25. *Pooh Corner (9+)* Pro: To 3".
26. *(10b TR)* Face just right of Pooh Corner.

8. TIGERS IN LIPSTICK FORMATION

Located 300 feet past dam on left side of road.
1.   Tigers in Lipstick (10a) ★   Pro: To 1.5".

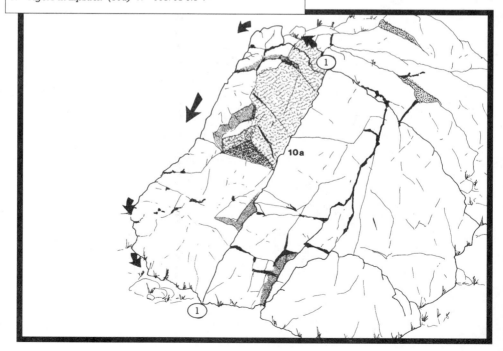

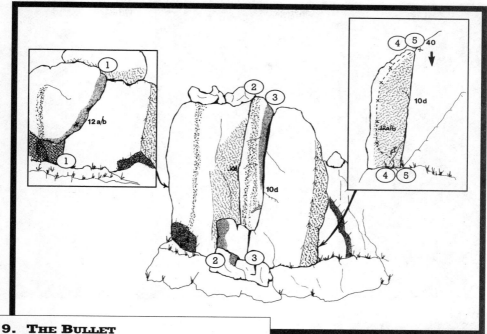

9. THE BULLET

1. *Finger Tattoo (12b)*   Pro: To 1".
2. *Pretty Blue Gun (12a)* ★★   Pro: To 2.5", extra #1-2.5".
3. *Where Eagles Die (11a)*   Pro: To 4.5", mostly big.
4. *Sharps 50 (12a/b)* ★★★   Pro: #1.5 and #2.
5. *Spy Dust (10d)* ★★   Pro: To 3.5".

**BUTTONROCK DAM AREA
BOULDERING WALL**

Located between Tigers in Lipstick formation and The Bullet.

SOUTH ST. VRAIN

"But I don't want to go among mad people," Alice remarked.
"Oh, you can't help that," said the Cat, "We're all mad here. I'm mad. You're mad."
"How do you know I'm mad?" said Alice.
"You must be," said the Cat, "or you wouldn't have come here."

Lewis Carroll
Alice in Wonderland

South St. Vrain canyon, located between the towns of Lyons and Allenspark on Highway 7, is an eleven mile long canyon filled with granite cliffs ranging in hieght from 40' to 400'. A great many of the rocks have had only the most obvious lines done, leaving plenty of room for newer, harder routes. Some of the rocks have probably not seen any climbing traffic at all.

There is a wide variety of climbing here, with climbs rated from 5.5 to 5.14 projects. Whereas the older climbs tend to follow obvious crack systems, the newer climbs tend to be bolt protected thin cracks or faces. Needless to say, there is a great deal of new route potential here, in all the grades. Not much is known about early exploration, but running across an old ring angle on what one judges to be a first ascent gives you an idea of how long climbers have been active in this area.

It wouldn't surprise me to find out that Layton Kor, Pat Ament, Larry Dalke and other active climbers of that era had put up many of the obvious climbs. Leonard Coyne, Roger and Bill Briggs, the Lowe Brothers, Gene Ellis, Steve Brodhead, Brett and Judy Ruckman, Tim Hunt and Tom Brown were responsible for many of the older climbs in this guide. Mark Rolofson, Paul Gagner, Alvino Pon, Hank Caylor and others have established many of the newer, harder routes.

THE ROCKS ARE DESCRIBED AS BEING EITHER ON THE RIGHT OR LEFT AS YOU ARE DRIVING UP THE CANYON FROM LYONS.

The following mileages are approximate and according to your own odometer. For best results, keep your eyes open and keep track of the formations until you reach your destination.

0.0 miles; Light at the junction of Highways 36 and 7 in Lyons. [GPS 0476883/4452693].

1- *Scout Rock...3.0 miles [GPS 0473603/4450413]*

2- *Guardian Rock...3.4 miles [GPS 0472989/4450384-parking] On left side just above the river. Known routes are on the upper west face.*

3- *The Mushroom Massif...3.8 miles [GPS 0472458/4450058- parking] The 400' formation on the left about 700 feet above the river.*

4- *Desdomona...3.85 miles First seperate formation west of The Mushroom Massiff on the same side of the river.*

5- *December Wall...4.3 miles Long formation on the right side, 800' above the road. All known routes start left of the large corner left of center (Winter Dream) and left of where the rocks become broken up*

The next three rock formations can all be reached from the large pullout directly across from The Sentinel.

6- *The Sentinel...4.5 miles [GPS 0471943/4449385] Just above the river on the left side.*

7- *Roadside Rock...4.6 miles [GPS 0471896/4449278] Right off of the road on the right side; first rock formation past the pullout.*

8- *Sweat Loaf...4.7 miles [GPS 0471809/4449117] 250' dome upstream from The Sentinel on the same side of the river.*

9- *Super Chunk...4.8 miles [GPS 0471891/4449393] Park in a pullout by the driveway to the summer cottages on the left. This rock is on the right side about 800' above the road. The following four rocks are all approached from the pullout directly across from Lower Infirmary Slab.*

10- *Lower Infirmary Slab...5.1 miles [GPS 0471680/4448491- parking] On the right side, but hard to see from the road. These slabs are about 300' above the road directly across from a small pullout on the south side.*

11- *Upper Infirmary Slab...Approach as for Lower Infirmary, but follow the trail around the front of the slab to the left. Go uphill through a small rock band, traversing back to the right,then uphill to the Upper Infirmary Slab.*

12- *Clinical Pinnacle...This is the small pinnacle even with the top of Lower Infirmary and about 200' west.*

13- *Left Infirmary Slab...Roughly 300' west of Clinical Pinnacle and about 300' above the road, this rock is characterized by a large roof on the left side. It is best approached by walking down the road to a quarried area, heading toward Observatory Rock, then uphill to the rock.*

14- *Observatory Rock...5.3 miles [GPS 0471380/4448303] On the right side just past the road to the ranger housing and immediately above a pullout.*

15- *Ye Olde Rock. This rock is located directly across from Observatory Rock, up the hill and across the river.*

16- *North Narrows Slab...5.4 miles Immediately off the road on the right side, just around the corner from Observatory Rock.*

17- *South Narrows Slabs...5.4 Miles Directly across the the river from North Narrows Slab on the left.*

18- *Vrain Dead Formation...Located on the same side of the road as North Narrows Slab, roughly 300' from the west end of North Narrows and about 200' uphill.*

The next three formations are all approached from the parking in the large pullout in front of Spire Rock.

19- *Spire Rock...6.0 miles [GPS 0470782/4447625-parking] Obvious seperate rock formation on the left side above the river.*

20- *Bullshit Rock...6.0 miles [GPS 0470782/4447625-parking] Located just above the river northeast of the pullout and downstream from Spire Rock.*

21- *The Wailing Wall...6.0 miles [GPS 0470782/4447625-parking] This formation is located on summit of the ridge north and east of the pullout.*

22- *Little Ogre...6.0 miles [GPS 0470589/4447508]Large formation on left side immediately above the river.*

23- *Monkey Skull...6.5 miles [GPS 0470102/4447641] On the right side about 200' above the road, characterized by the large right facing corner on the west face (Sunshine Dihedral). Approach is best made from the smaller pullout on the right side below the indistinct east face.Beware of Poison Ivy on the trail and at the base of the cliff.*

24- *Trojan Bunny Buttress...7.2 miles [GPS 0469608/4447557- parking] Large formation with many roofs about 400' above the river on the left.*

25- *Leatherface...7.2 miles 150' farther, next west facing slab.*

26- *Acrophile Rock...7.6 miles This rock is located east and north of the large pullout on the left side of the road about 1000' uphill.*

27- *Hideaway Dome...8.7 miles [GPS 0467514/4446518-parking] Located up a valley about 1000 feet above the river on the left side.*

28- *The Fang...9.1 miles [GPS 0466593/4446464-parking] Prominent buttress 600 feet above the river on the left side.Park in a pullout on the left side of the road underneath the buttress. Walk west until you get to a small bridge.Cross the river, going left up a 4x4 road for about 20 minutes.At an eroded area on the right, pick up a trail that goes up the north side of a canyon, passing an old mine, to reach the south face of The Fang. Walk north along the west face to reach the climbs. This approach is about 40 minutes long.*

29- *Violator Buttress...9.6 miles [GPS 0466183/4446460] 100 feet off of the road on the right side immediately north of a two track pullout and just before an abandoned cabin.*

30- *The Watchtower...10.4 miles [GPS 0464687/4446918] Last formation in the canyon on the left side. Characterized by the large corner that splits the formation (Watchtower Corner).*

31- *The Piz Badille...Located about 2.5 miles down Highway 72 (Peak to Peak Highway) on the left side just before you reach Peaceful Valley.*

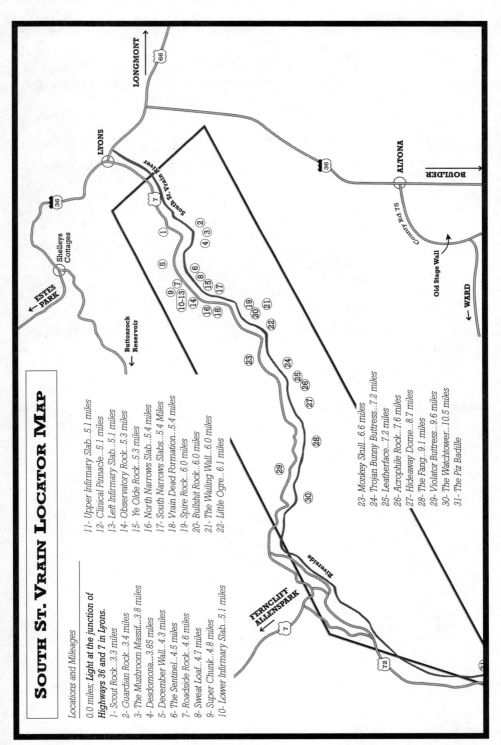

South St. Vrain Locator Map

Locations and Mileages

0.0 miles; **Light at the junction of Highways 36 and 7 in Lyons.**

1- Scout Rock...3.3 miles
2- Guardian Rock...3.4 miles
3- The Mushroom Massif...3.8 miles
4- Desdomona...3.85 miles
5- December Wall...4.3 miles
6- The Sentinel...4.5 miles
7- Roadside Rock...4.6 miles
8- Sweat Loaf...4.7 miles
9- Super Chunk...4.8 miles
10- Lower Infirmary Slab...5.1 miles

11- Upper Infirmary Slab...5.1 miles
12- Clinical Pinnacle...5.1 miles
13- Left Infirmary Slab...5.1 miles
14- Observatory Rock...5.3 miles
15- Ye Olde Rock...5.3 miles
16- North Narrows Slab...5.4 miles
17- South Narrows Slabs...5.4 miles
18- Vrain Dead Formation...5.4 miles
19- Spire Rock...6.0 miles
20- Bullshit Rock...6.0 miles
21- The Wailing Wall...6.0 miles
22- Little Ogre...6.1 miles

23- Monkey Skull...6.6 miles
24- Trojan Bunny Buttress...7.2 miles
25- Leatherface...7.2 miles
26- Acrophile Rock...7.6 miles
27- Hideaway Dome...8.7 miles
28- The Fang...9.1 miles
29- Violator Buttress...9.6 miles
30- The Watchtower...10.5 miles
31- The Piz Badille

1. SCOUT ROCK

1. **Unknown**   *Goes over roof with bolts to a right leaning crack.*
2. **Unknown**   *30 feet right of previous route. Follows right lean-ing seam with bolts to anchors. Bolts are currently without hangers.*

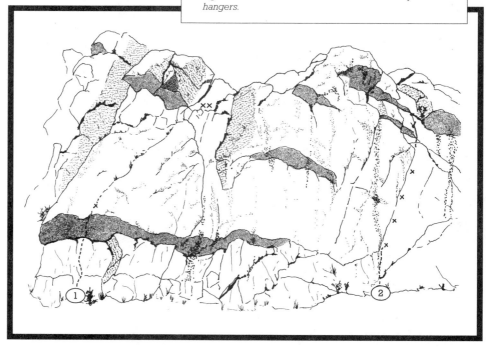

2. GUARDIAN ROCK

1. *Shuffling Madness* (11b) ★★★
   Pro: To 3".
2. *Weight of the World* (11b) ★★
   Pro: to 2".

3. THE MUSHROOM MASSIF

Note: Due to some inconsistent and incomplete information on this rock, climbs here should be treated as first ascents and bolt gear is advisable. Anchors may or may not be where indicated and ratings may be different than shown.

1. Stone Knives   (12a) ★★   Pro: To 4".
2. Coldwater Drama (9)   Pro: To 4".
3. Ice Hose Route (WI4+)
4. Sego Conspiracy (7)   Pro: To 4".
5. Pollemor (8) ★   Pro: To 4".
6. Unknown (7)   Pro: To 4".
7. The Mushroom (8) ★★   Pro: Miscellaneous to 2".

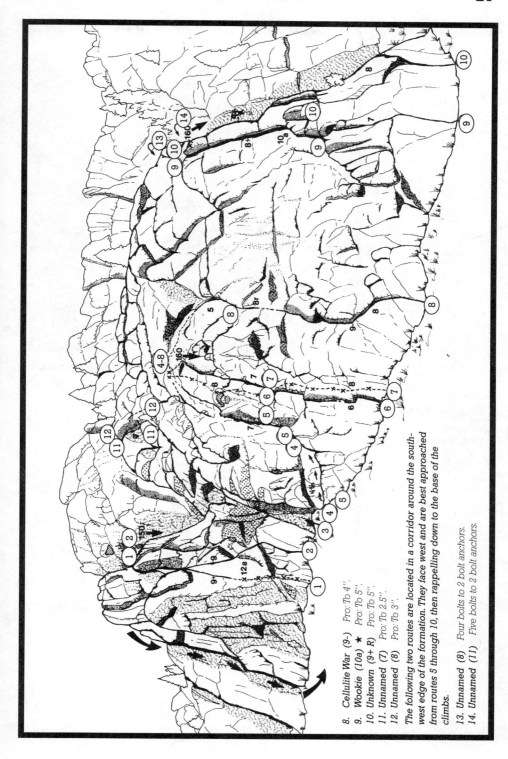

8. *Cellulite War (9-)* Pro: To 4''.
9. *Wookie (10a)* ★ Pro: To 5''.
10. *Unknown (9+ R)* Pro: To 5''.
11. *Unnamed (7)* Pro: To 2.5''.
12. *Unnamed (8)* Pro: To 3''.

The following two routes are located in a corridor around the south-west edge of the formation. They face west and are best approached from routes 5 through 10, then rappelling down to the base of the climbs.

13. *Unnamed (8)* Four bolts to 2 bolt anchors.
14. *Unnamed (11)* Five bolts to 2 bolt anchors.

4. DESDOMONA

1. *North Face (10c/d)* ★★   *Pro: To 4″.*
2. *North Face Variation (9)* ★   *Pro: To 4″, extra 3″ - 4″.*

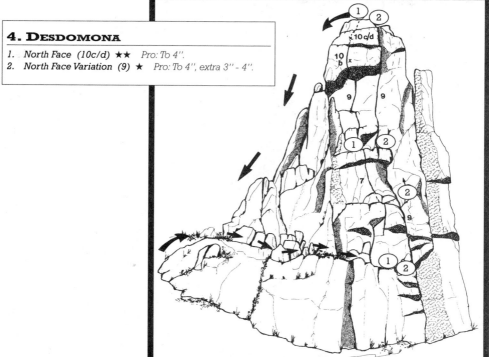

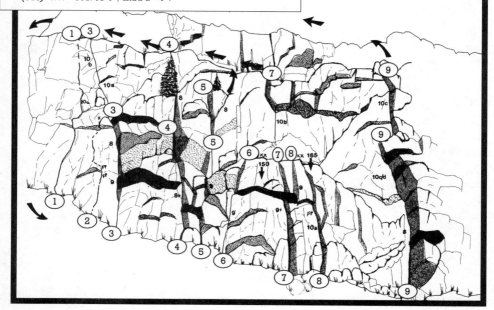

5. DECEMBER WALL

Note: All known climbs start from the large corner left of center, and left of where the rock becomes broken up. Due to some inconsistent and incomplete information on this rock, climbs here should be treated as first ascents and bolt gear is advisable. Anchors may or may not be where indicated and ratings may be different than shown.

1. **Unnamed (10a/b)** *Pro: To 4".*
2. **Unnamed (10a)** *Pro: To 4".*
3. **I Promise Not To Cam In Your Mouth (10b)** *Pro: To 4".*
4. **Great Tree Route (8+)** ★ *Pro: To 4".*
5. **Short Takes (9)** *Pro: To 4".*
6. **I'm Camming, I'm Camming (9)** *Pro: To 4", extra thin.*
7. **Caesar's Crack (10b)** ★ *Pro: To 4", extra thin.*
8. **Ranklands of Infinity (10b)** ★ *Pro: To 4", extra thin.*
9. **Winter Dreams aka Gene and George's Excellent Adventure (10c)** ★★ *Pro: To 4", extra 2"-4".*

6. THE SENTINEL

1. *Spy Story (8/9)*   Pro: To 4".
2. *I Spy (8+ R)*   Pro: To 3.5".
3. *Tapestry (9-)*   Pro: To 4".
4. *Roundabout (9-)*   Pro: To 3".
5. *Crooked Cross (9+)* ★★★   Pro: To 3".
6. *Southern Cross (10a)* ★   Pro: To 3".

7. ROADSIDE ROCK

1. *Left Side* *(8)* ★   *Pro: To 4"*
2. *Open Project (12d/13a?)*   *Toprope.*
3. *Unknown (9+)* ★   *Pro: To 3.5".*

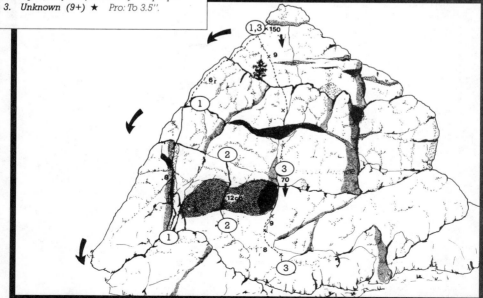

8. SWEAT LOAF

1. *Independent Worm Saloon (10c)* ★★   *Pro: To 2'', extra wires.*
2. *Gravity's Rainbow (11b)* ★★★   *Pro: To 2.5'', include small cams.*

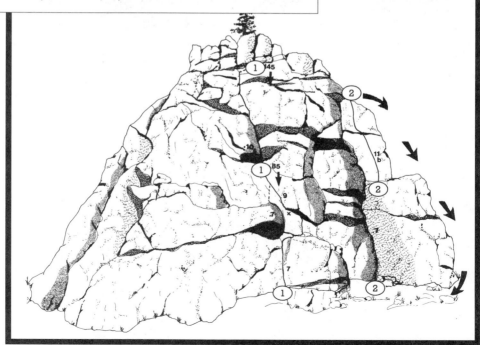

9. SUPERCHUNK

1. *Man Bites Dog (10b)* ★   *Pro: To 2", extra medium wires.*
2. *Open Project (13)*   *Toprope arête.*
3. *Hairway To Steven (11a)* ★★   *Pro: To 2".*

INFIRMARY SLAB AREA AND NARROWS AREA OVERVIEW

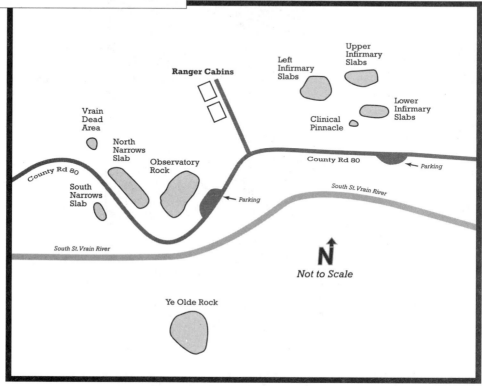

10. LOWER INFIRMARY SLABS

See overview on previous page.

10. Acts of Contrition *(9+)*
11. Plague Boys *(7)*
12. Morning Oyster *(6)*   *Pro: Miscellaneous to 2.5".*

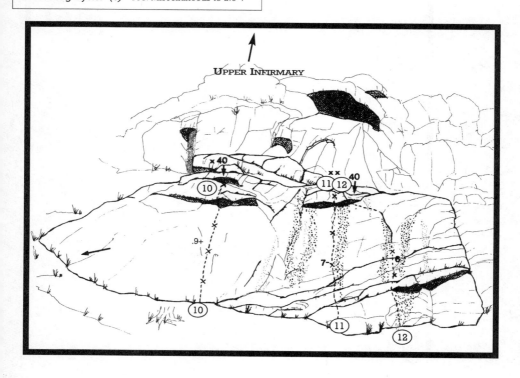

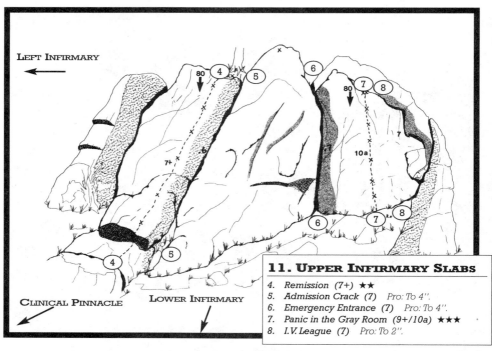

11. UPPER INFIRMARY SLABS

4. *Remission (7+)* ★★
5. *Admission Crack (7)*   Pro: To 4".
6. *Emergency Entrance (7)*   Pro: To 4".
7. *Panic in the Gray Room (9+/10a)* ★★★
8. *I.V. League (7)*   Pro: To 2".

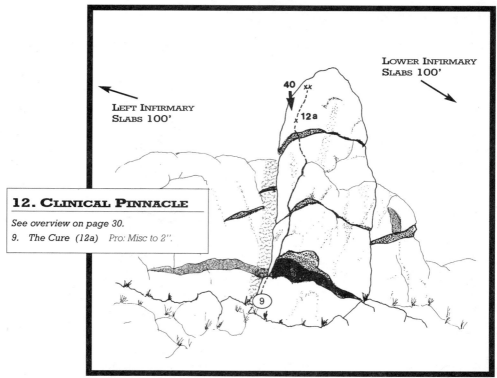

12. CLINICAL PINNACLE

See overview on page 30.
9. *The Cure (12a)*   Pro: Misc to 2".

13. Left Infirmary Slabs

See overview on page 30.

1. *Unknown Slab Route* *(8+ R)* *Pro: To 3".*
2. *Dipshit Boss* *(8+ R)* *Pro: To 3".*
3. *Wax 'n' Wane* *(8+ R)* *Pro: To 2".*

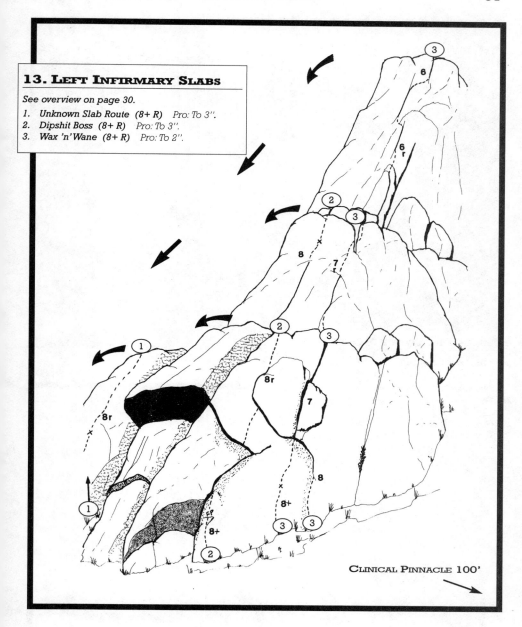

CLINICAL PINNACLE 100'

14. OBSERVATORY ROCK

See overview on page 30.

18. *Killer Instinct (12c/d)* ★★★   *Pro: Misc to 3''.*
19. *Skin Mechanic (10a/b)* ★   *Pro: To 2''.*
20. *The Glass Bead Game (11a)* ★★   *Pro: To 2''.*
21. *99% Pure (8)*   *Pro: To 4''.*
22. *Original Route (8)* ★   *Pro: To 4''.*
23. *Wilford Roof (12b)*   *Pro: To 3.5'', #10 hex.*

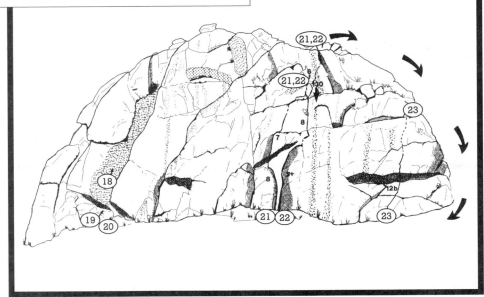

14. OBSERVATORY ROCK SOUTH SIDE

See overview on page 30.

18.   *Killer Instinct (12c/d)* ★★★   *Pro: Misc to 3".*
18a. *Unknown (12+?)*
19.   *Skin Mechanic (10a/b)* ★   *Pro: To 2".*
20.   *The Glass Bead Game (11a)* ★★   *Pro: To 2".*
21.   *99% Pure (8)*   *Pro: To 4".*
22.   *Original Route (8)* ★   *Pro: To 4".*

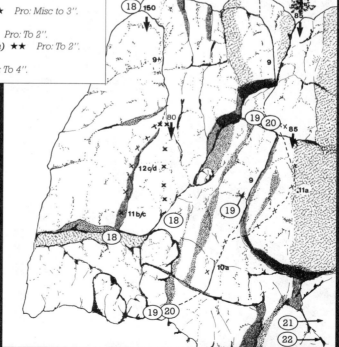

15. Ye Olde Rock

See overview on page 30.

1.   *Forgotten Passage* *(9)* ★   *Pro: To 4".*

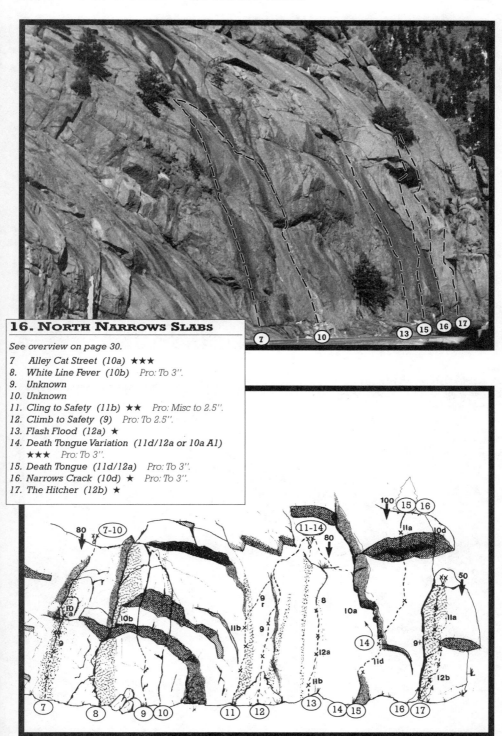

16. NORTH NARROWS SLABS

See overview on page 30.

7   Alley Cat Street (10a) ★★★
8. White Line Fever (10b)   *Pro: To 3".*
9. Unknown
10. Unknown
11. Cling to Safety (11b) ★★   *Pro: Misc to 2.5".*
12. Climb to Safety (9)   *Pro: To 2.5".*
13. Flash Flood (12a) ★
14. Death Tongue Variation (11d/12a or 10a A1)
    ★★★   *Pro: To 3".*
15. Death Tongue (11d/12a)   *Pro: To 3".*
16. Narrows Crack (10d) ★   *Pro: To 3".*
17. The Hitcher (12b) ★

17. SOUTH NARROWS SLABS

See overview on page 30.

2. *Sidetrack (6)*   *Pro: To 1".*
3. *Pon Scum (12a/b)* ★   *Pro: QDs.*
4. *Bullfight (13b)* ★★   *Pro: QDs.*

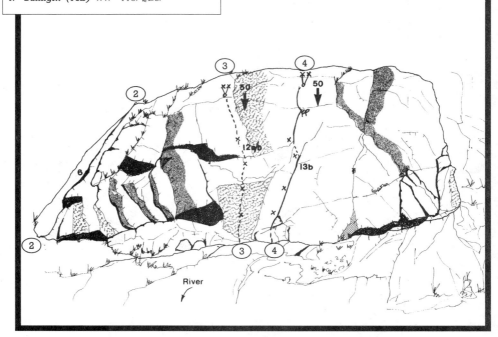

18. The Narrows Area
Vrain Dead Formation

See overview on page 30.

5. **Vrain Child** *(11c/d or 11a)* ★ *Pro: QDs and midsize stopper.*
6. **Vrain Dead** *(8+)* *Pro: To 4".*

SOUTH ST. VRAIN OVERVIEW DETAIL

BULLSHIT ROCK

4. Bullshit Detector (9 or 11a)   *Pro: To 1", many wires.*

THE WAILING WALL

1. The North Corner (10b) ★   *Pro: To 3".*
3. The Three Stigmata (10c)   *Pro: To 2.5".*

SPIRE ROCK

1. Full Nelson Reilly (10c) ★★   *Pro: To 2.5".*
2. Dire Spire (9-)   *Pro: To 3".*
3. Higher Spire (8) ★   *Pro: To 3".*
4. Blow Chow (8)   *Pro: To 3".*

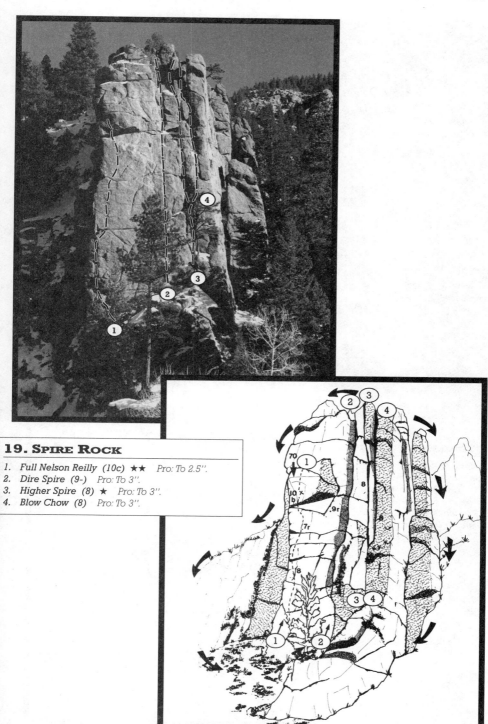

19. SPIRE ROCK

1. *Full Nelson Reilly (10c)* ★★   *Pro: To 2.5".*
2. *Dire Spire (9-)*   *Pro: To 3".*
3. *Higher Spire (8)* ★   *Pro: To 3".*
4. *Blow Chow (8)*   *Pro: To 3".*

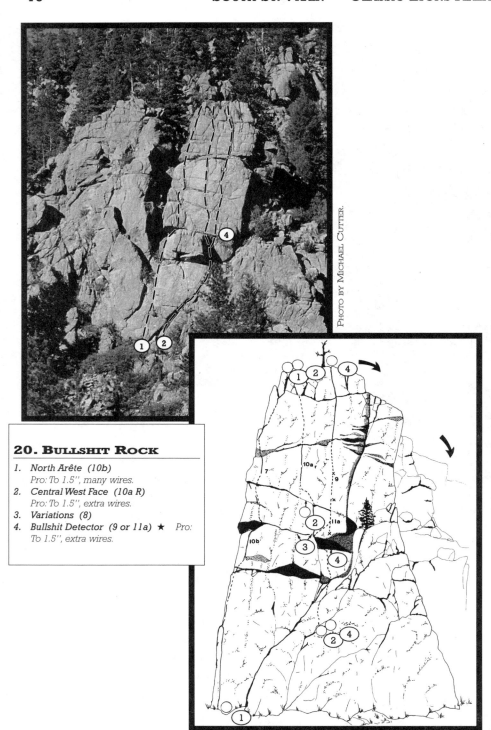

PHOTO BY MICHAEL CUTTER.

20. BULLSHIT ROCK

1. **North Arête** *(10b)*
   Pro: To 1.5″, many wires.
2. **Central West Face** *(10a R)*
   Pro: To 1.5″, extra wires.
3. **Variations** *(8)*
4. **Bullshit Detector** *(9 or 11a)* ★   *Pro: To 1.5″, extra wires.*

Photo by Michael Cutter.

21. THE WAILING WALL

1. *The North Corner (10b)* ★   Pro: To 3".
2. *The Wages of Sin (11d)* ★★★   Pro: To 1"; to 3" for the North Corner finish.
3. *The Three Stigmata (10c)* ★★   Pro: To 3.5".

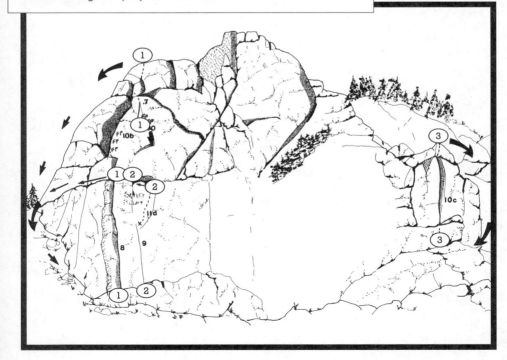

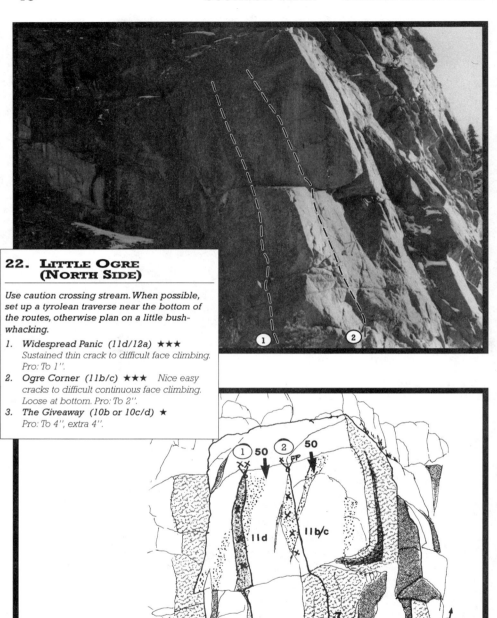

22. LITTLE OGRE (NORTH SIDE)

Use caution crossing stream. When possible, set up a tyrolean traverse near the bottom of the routes, otherwise plan on a little bush-whacking.

1. **Widespread Panic (11d/12a) ★★★**
   Sustained thin crack to difficult face climbing. Pro: To 1".
2. **Ogre Corner (11b/c) ★★★**   *Nice easy cracks to difficult continuous face climbing. Loose at bottom. Pro: To 2".*
3. **The Giveaway (10b or 10c/d) ★**
   Pro: To 4", extra 4".

22. Little Ogre

1. **Widespread Panic** *(11d/12a)* ★★★
   Pro: To 1''.
2. **Ogre Corner** *(11b/c)* ★★★
   Pro: To 2''.
3. **The Giveaway** *(10b or 10c/d)* ★
   Pro: To 4''.
4. **Unknown** *(11b)* *Pro: To 2.5''.*

23. MONKEY SKULL

23. Monkey Skull

The bolt hangers keep disappearing from some of these nice routes. It's best to bring some hangers with you or plan on threading stoppers on some of the bolt studs.

1. Crack (9-) *Pro: To 2.5".*
2. Amy, Good Gorilla (10b/c) *Pro: To 2".*
3. Casual Corner (8+) *Pro: To 2".*
4. Fringe Dweller (10c) ★★ *Pro: #0 or #1 TCU.*
5. Hollow Be Thy Name (10d/11a) ★★ *Reach. Pro: To 2.5".*
6. Sunshine Dihedral (10a/b) ★★★ *Pro: To 4".*
7. Alvino's Variation (9) *Pro: To 4".*
8. Upside The Cranium (10a/b) ★★★★
9. Fever Dance (10c) ★★ *Pro: To 2.5".*
10. Fever Dance Variation (9) ★ *Pro: To 3.5".*
11. Summit Block (10a) *Pro: To 2".*

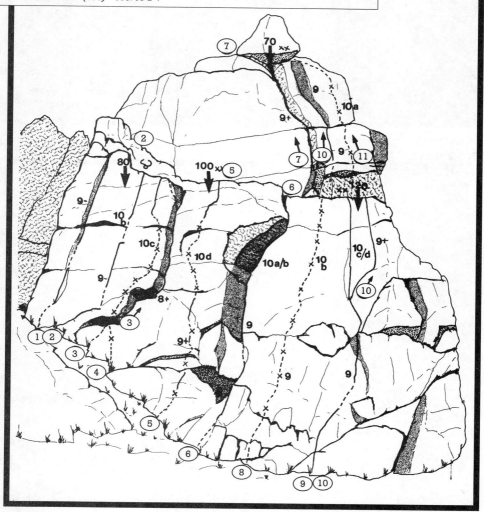

24. TROJAN BUNNY BUTTRESS (EAST FACE)

1. Project (?)

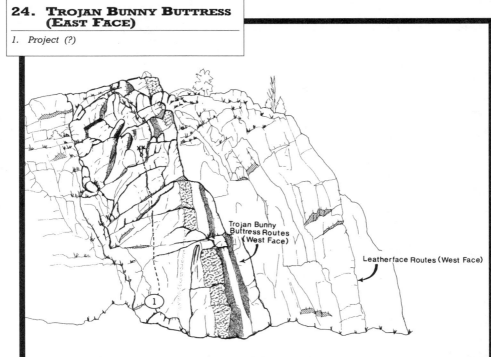

Trojan Bunny
Buttress Routes
(West Face)

Leatherface Routes (West Face)

24. TROJAN BUNNY BUTTRESS (WEST FACE)

1. *Project (?)*
2. *Lick My Plate (8+)* ★ *Pro: To 1".*
3. *Streatch (9+)* *Pro: To 1".*
4. *Dog Will Hunt (10b)* *Pro: To 2".*
5. *Unknown (?)* *Very clean crack through roofs.*

25. LEATHERFACE

6. *Project (?)* *Fingercrack.*
7. *Vrain Storm (9 R/X)* *Pro: To 1.5".*
8. *Pondemonium (10d)* ★★★
9. *Shake 'n' Bake (8)* *Pro: To 3".*
10. *Serendipity (7)* ★ *Pro: To 3".*

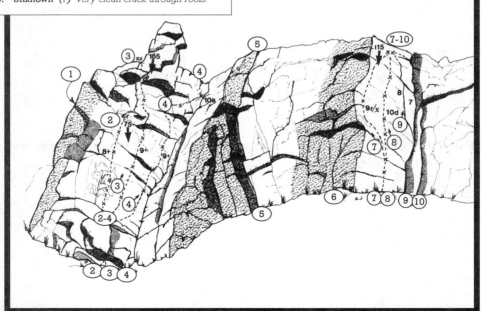

26. ACROPHILE ROCK

1. *Acrophilia (11a)* ★★　*Pro: To 4".*
2. *Acrophilia Direct (11b)*　*Pro: To 4".*

27. HIDEAWAY DOME

1. *Gumby Parade (11a)* ★★   *Pro: To 3.5".*
2. *Hidden Pleasures (8+)*   *Pro: To 4".*

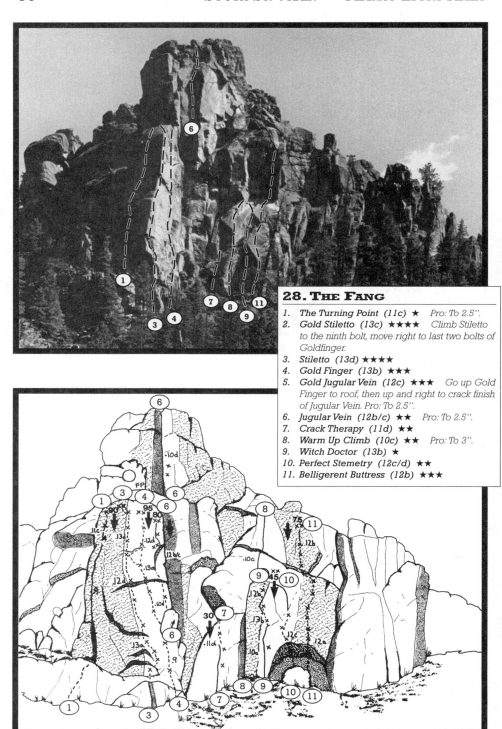

28. THE FANG

1. **The Turning Point** *(11c)* ★ *Pro: To 2.5".*
2. **Gold Stiletto** *(13c)* ★★★★ *Climb Stiletto to the ninth bolt, move right to last two bolts of Goldfinger.*
3. **Stiletto** *(13d)* ★★★★
4. **Gold Finger** *(13b)* ★★★
5. **Gold Jugular Vein** *(12c)* ★★★ *Go up Gold Finger to roof, then up and right to crack finish of Jugular Vein. Pro: To 2.5".*
6. **Jugular Vein** *(12b/c)* ★★ *Pro: To 2.5".*
7. **Crack Therapy** *(11d)* ★★
8. **Warm Up Climb** *(10c)* ★★ *Pro: To 3".*
9. **Witch Doctor** *(13b)* ★
10. **Perfect Stemetry** *(12c/d)* ★★
11. **Belligerent Buttress** *(12b)* ★★★

29. Violator Buttress

1. *Trespassers Will Be Violated (11b/c)*   Pro: To 2.5".
2. *The Violator (10a)*   Pro: To 4".

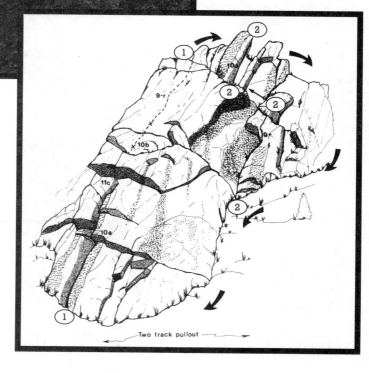

30. THE WATCHTOWER

1. *Watchtower Corner (9-)* ★   *Pro: To 4".*
2. *Highway Robbery (11b or 12a)* ★★★
3. *Business Loop (11b)* ★★

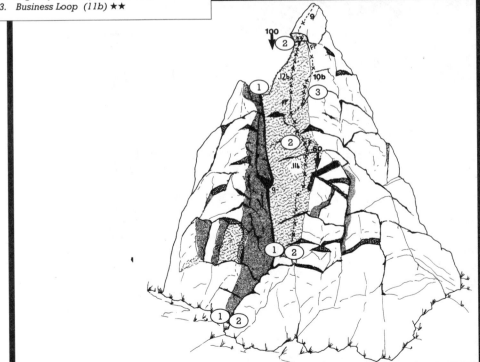

ED GERET LEADING FIRST ASCENT OF *FEVER DANCE* 'NOTE THE EBS'!
PHOTO BY JEFFERY BUTTERFIELD.

31. THE PIZ BADILLE

1. *The Ridge (6)* ★★ *Pro: To 4".*
2. *Bad Badille (7+)* *Pro: To 4".*
3. *The Great Escapade (8 R)* *Pro: To 4".*
4. *Reusable Love Bag (9+)* ★★ *Pro: To 2".*
5. *Too Many Puppies (9-)* ★★ *Pro: To 2".*
6. *Escape from Zonerland (9+)* *Pro: To 2".*
7. *Unknown (9+)* *Pro: To 3".*
8. *Southwest Face (7 R)* *Pro: To 3".*
9. *Sympathetic Mind Fuck (6)* ★★ *Pro: Misc to 2".*

ED GERET LEADING *SUNSHINE DIHEDRAL*
5.10A/B ★★ ON THE MONKEY SKULL.
PHOTO BY JEFFERY BUTTERFIELD.

OLD STAGE WALL
AREA CLOSED!

Since the publication of Richard Rossiter's book Boulder Climbs North 1988, this beautiful climbing area has been closed. This area is on private land and the landowner became worried about the liability issues, a prime and sad example of what is happening (at a very alarming rate) across the states. This area has been included for two reasons. 1. To give the Access Fund a little more ammunition in their efforts to reopen the area by establishing a historical use. 2. To make climbers more aware of the fact that this is indeed happening in Colorado. Please become more involved with access issues including: not crossing private land, trash, noise and disrupting traffic. This information has been included here for historical purposes and is not presented to be used as route information for climbing and does not give permission to climb here or trespass on this land. Please respect the closure. By climbing here, you will only further damage relations with the landowners and jeopardize the re-opening of this area to climbing.

OLD STAGE WALL

1. *Dragon Lady (12b/c)*
2. *Via Dolorosa "Sorrowful Road" (11b/c A0)*
3. *Alex in Wonderland (11d)*
4. *Trojan Crack (11b)* Pro: To 2.5".
5. *The Solstice (13a)*
6. *Flying Saucers (12a)*
7. *Unnamed (12 TR)*

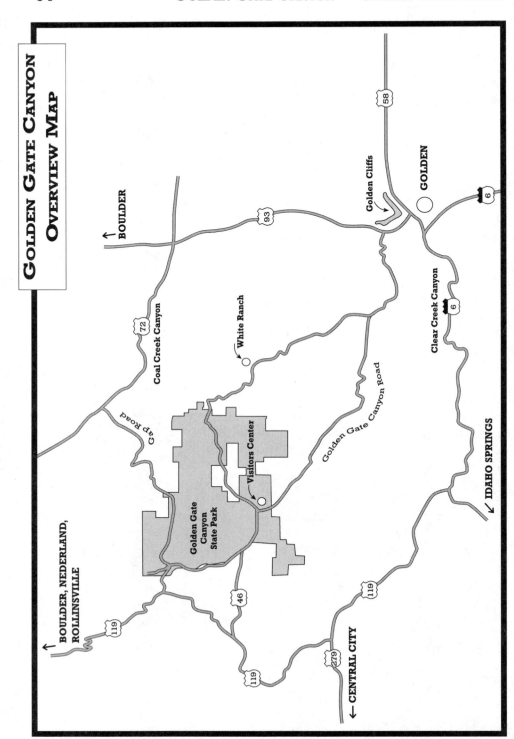

GOLDEN GATE CANYON
OVERVIEW MAP

GOLDEN GATE CANYON STATE PARK

"Have some wine," said the March Hare in an encouraging tone.
Alice looked all round the table, but there was nothing on it but tea.
"I don't see any wine," she remarked.
"There isn't any," said the March Hare.

Lewis Carroll
Alice in Wonderland

Golden Gate Canyon State Park, located west of Golden, is filled with a multitude of granite formations up to 500' high. The granite resembles that found in Boulder Canyon, but is rougher and more alpine in nature. The elevations of most of the rocks are fairly high, between 8,000 and 10,000 feet. This makes for some very nice, cool summer climbing in a very accessible area.

Of all the formations that abound in Golden Gate, only the ones with known climbing are included in this guide. This is yet another area where a great deal of the climbing history has been lost. People have been climbing here since the early '50s and climbs of some technical difficulty exist on almost every rock formation. The only evidence of these early ascents exists in the form of the occassional fixed pin or pin scar.

As this is a very alpine area, weather is a serious consideration, and, coupled with some lengthy approaches, is well worth planning for. Most of the weather moves in from the west and is usually pretty obvious.

The approaches for the climbs range from 20 to 60 minutes with most of the approaches being somewhere in between. The climbs range in difficulty from 5.2 to mid–5.11. Most of the climbs follow natural crack lines with the occassional fixed pin or bolt. There are a few bolted faces and most of these take some additional gear. **There is an abundance of new route potential in this area.**

DIRECTIONS   From the junction of Colorado Highway 58 and I-70, go west on CO 58, passing under Golden Cliffs, to the junction of Colorado Highway 93 and US Hwy 6. Turn right (north) on Hwy 93 for 1.4 miles and turn left (west) onto Golden Gate Canyon Road. Follow this for 15 miles to the park entrance.

From Boulder, take Hwy 93 south to the Golden Gate Canyon Road and turn right (west).

A $3.00 daily use fee or a state parks pass is required.

CAMPING AND RECREATION   This is a very pretty park and is a nice area to bring non–climbers. There is a multitude of hiking trails, bike trails, fishing and cross country skiing, and picnic areas with water fountains.

As you turn onto Golden Gate Canyon Road you will come to a right turn with a sign for White Ranch. White Ranch Park has some of the best mountain bike trails close to Boulder and Denver and is well worth checking out.

To reach the climbs on Ralston Roost and Son of Ralston: From the visitor's center, turn left, heading toward Kriley Pond. The first parking area that you will come to is on your left at Slough Pond. You may park here and pick up a trail that will take you to the saddle between the two rocks. This is the harder of the two ways to approach these rocks. Suit yourself.

The easiest approach is to drive to the road that is just past Kriley Pond and take a right turn, following the road to a circular driveway and parking lot. A shorter trail leaves this lot and curves under the south face of Ralston Roost. Take a fainter climbers trail toward the rocks when the main trail starts to turn away from them.

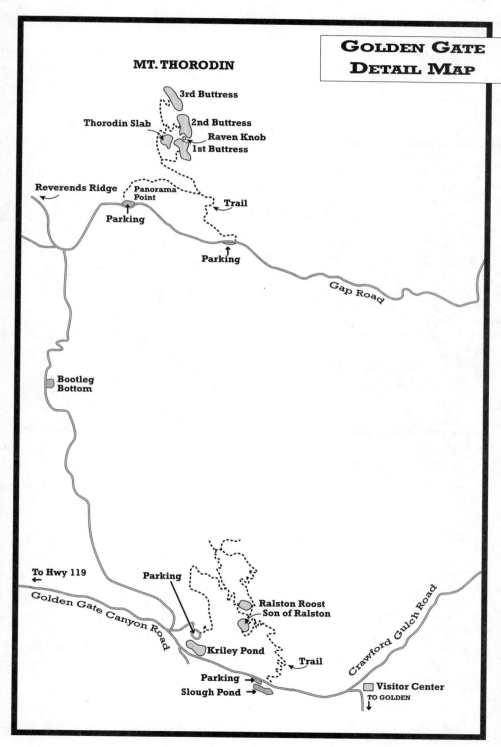

GOLDEN GATE
DETAIL MAP

MT. THORODIN

3rd Buttress

Thorodin Slab
2nd Buttress

Raven Knob
1st Buttress

Reverends Ridge
Panorama
Point

Trail

Parking

Parking

Gap Road

Bootleg
Bottom

To Hwy 119

Parking

Golden Gate Canyon Road

Ralston Roost
Son of Ralston

Crawford Gulch Road

Kriley Pond

Trail

Parking

Slough Pond

Visitor Center
TO GOLDEN

SON OF RALSTON

1. **Unknown (10a/b)**   *The leftmost of the thin cracks on the west wall. 2 bolts at top of pitch 2 where crack ends. Two-bolt anchor. Pro: To 2".*
2. **Son of Purina (9+)**   *Pro: To 3".*
3. **Nomad's Land (7+)**   *Pro: To 3.5".*

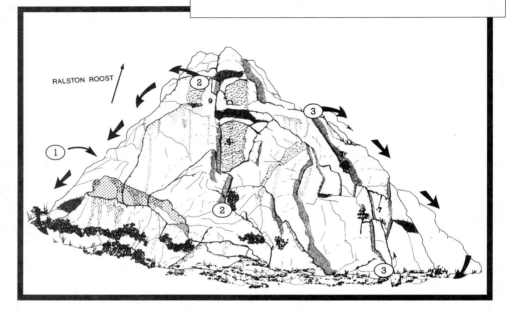

RALSTON ROOST

1. *West Face Route* *(8)* *Pro: To 3".*
2. *Gene's Route* *(11a/b R)* *Pro: To 3".*
3. *Pilly the Pimp* *(10a)* *Pro: To 3", extra 2-3".*
4. *Southside Corner* *(10b)* *Pro: To 4".*
5. *Rain Fuck* *(11a)* *Pro: To 4".*
6. *Brewski* *(10a)* *Pro: To 4".*
7. *Bangyerded* *(9)* *Pro: To 3".*

GENE ELLIS ON *MR. MISTY* 5.10A
MOUNT THORODIN, SECOND BUTTRESS.

MOUNT THORODIN

All of the rocks in this area are approached by the same main trail and only deviate as you get closer to the separate formations.

From the visitors center, go left, following the signs to Kriley Pond. At Kriley pond, turn right, and follow the road to Panorama Point. Park here. Directly across the valley as you are looking to the north are three major rock formations. From right to left they are: The First, Second and Third Buttresses. Thorodin Slab is the lower slab between the First and Second Buttress, and Raven Knob is the high point on the ridge just above that.

Take the Racoon trail from Panorama Point. This trail heads almost due east out of the parking lot and parrallels the main road for awhile before dropping down into the valley. It will curve back around and start heading west again, taking you underneath the First Buttress (way underneath.) Watch for the first left switchback. Here there is a faint trail heading straight off the switchback to the right. Take this trail as it goes west until you reach a faint open area about 900' below the Second Buttress. Turn uphill and follow a series of cairns and trail markings until you reach a scree field.

To reach The First Buttress, go right across the scree to the base of the rock. For Thorodin Slab, continue straight uphill from the scree. To approach The Second and Third Buttresses, look for cairns and markings that mark a trail that goes up and left.

Stay on this trail until you reach the scree field at the bottom of The Second Buttress. Stay to the right of the scree until almost even with the base of the rock before crossing over.

Allow at least an hour for both the approach and return trip back to your car.

MT. THORODIN : THIRD BUTTRESS

1.   *Explorer Scout* **(9)**   Pro: To 3.5″.

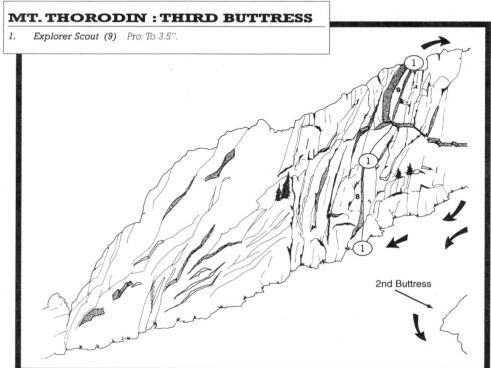

Raven Knob

RAVEN KNOB

15. Descent Route (2 X)
16. Ellis-Galbraith Route (8 R)
     Pro: misc. to 3".

MT. THORODIN: SECOND BUTTRESS

2. Northwest Ridge (7)   Pro: To 4".
3. Rick's Respite (6)   Pro: To 4".
4. Outland (9+)   Pro: To 3".
5. For Love of Mothernot (9)   Pro: To 3".
6. CMC Route (7)   Pro: To 4".
7. Papal Bull (9+)   Pro: To 3".

8.   Mr. Misty (10a)   Pro: To 3.5".
9.   The Choir Boys (10b)   Pro: To 3".
10. Pope on Dope (11a/b)   Pro: To 3".
11. Pope on a Rope (10a/b R)   Pro: To 3".
12. Gorilla's Delimna (9)   Pro: To 4", extra 2-3".
13. Rubble Ramble (9 R)   Pro: To 4".
14. Sirocco (8)   Pro: To 4".

3rd Buttress

2nd Buttress

RAVEN KNOB

15.   *Descent Route (2 X)*
16.   *Ellis-Galbraith Route (8 R)*   Pro: misc. to 3''.

THORODIN SLAB

17.   *Biege Spider (6)*   Pro: To 3''.

MT. THORODIN : FIRST BUTTRESS

18. *Twin Cracks* (8)   *Pro: To 4".*
19. *Twin Cracks Escape* (4)
20. *Twin Cracks Variation* (7)   *Start. Pro: To 4".*
21. *Padding About* (5)   *Pro: To 4".*

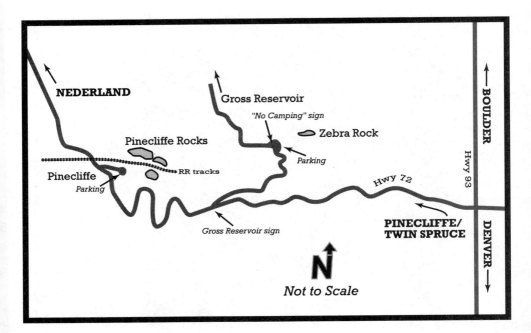

GROSS RESERVOIR AREA

The Queen had only one way of settling all difficulties, great or small. "Off with his head!", she said without even looking around.

Lewis Carroll
Alice in Wonderland

ZEBRA ROCK AND PINECLIFFE

These two areas are located just south of Boulder and west on CO 72. Most of the climbs are on granite formations about 100 feet high. The granite, as a whole, is pretty good and is a nice mixture of crack and face climbs. To get to Zebra Rock, drive to the junction of CO 93 and CO 72. Follow CO 72 towards Pinecliffe and Twin Spruce for 8 miles to Gross Reservoir. Turn right and drive an additional 3.2 miles until you see a white "No Camping" sign on your right. Park and follow a faint trail past the sign northeast for about 300 feet. Zebra Rock is on the east side of the ridge facing south.

For Pinecliffe, follow CO 72 an additional 5 miles past Gross Reservoir. Just after crossing the bridge east of Pinecliffe, turn right onto a dirt road that parallels the railroad tracks to a parking area. The main climbing rock is visible about 400 yards east on the north side of the tracks.

Dave Rice and Chris Scanlon were responsible for discovering, cleaning and climbing the climbs on Zebra Rock in 1988. John Loren and Les Schafer put up the early routes on Pinecliffe in 1987 with Alvino Pon, Eddie Pain and Z. Pomtier putting in the newer, harder routes.

CAMPING AND RECREATION   Camping is restricted to specific sites around Gross Reservoir. Some excellent mountain biking trails are found in the Walker Ranch areas as well as some very nice hiking. Excellent fishing can be found around the Pinecliffe area in the river that runs through town.

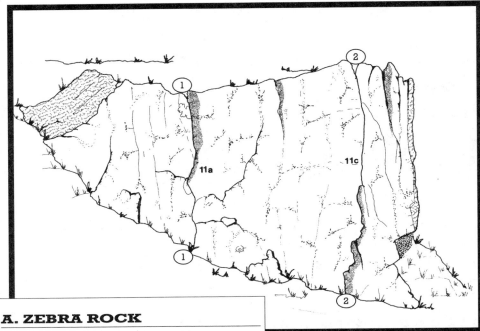

A. ZEBRA ROCK

1. *Earthbound Misfit (11a)*   Pro: To 4''.
2. *Zebra Crack aka Glitter Leopard (11c)*   Pro: To 2''.

B.PINECLIFFE AREA (NORTH SIDE CLIFFS)

1. **Hardman Jr. (11b/c)**   *Four bolts to 2-bolt anchor.*
2. **Knuckle Sandwich (10+)**   *Face to crack, clip first bolt on Pica. Pro: 1''-3''.*
3. **Pica (12)**   *Four bolts to 2-bolt anchor.*
4. **End of the Line (9)**   *Leads to Don't Blame the Youth. Pro: To 2.5''.*
5. **Don't Blame the Youth (12/13?)**   *Project.*
6. **Grimlock (9+)**   *Pro: To 2.5''.*
7. **Goldilocks (6)**   *Leads to Nocturnal Leg Muscle Cramp. Pro: To 2''.*
8. **Nocturnal Leg Muscle Cramp (11a)**   *One-pin, 4 bolts to 2-bolt anchor.*
9. **Blaster (11a)**   *Pro: To 2''.*
10. **Project**
11. **Frenzy (10a)**   *Pro: To 3.5''.*
12. **Crescent Moon (8)**   *Pro: To 3''.*
13. **Longhaired Freaky People (10a)**   *Five bolts to 2-bolt anchor.*

The following two routes are located on the cliff south of the railroad tracks but are not shown in topo format.

14. **Wimpy I (7 R)**   *Pro: To 3''.*
15. **Percepter (9)**   *Cross overhang to a large flake, follow finger crack through roof. Pro: To 2.5''.*

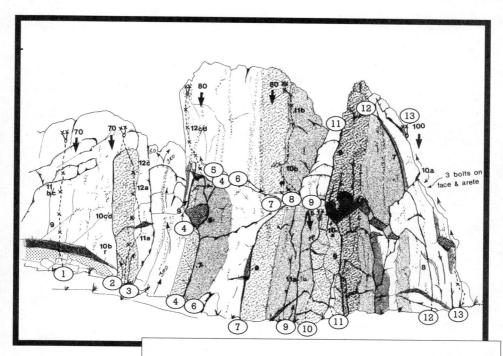

PINECLIFFE AREA (North side cliffs)

ROUTES BY GRADE

5.2 — 5.5

Descent Route (2 X)	73, 74
Rock Biter (3)	8
Twin Cracks Escape (4)	75
Padding About (5)	75

5.6

Biege Spider	74
First Door	8
Goldilocks	79
Morning Oyster	35
Rick's Respite	73
Ridge, The ★★	61
Sidetrack	42
Sympathetic Mind Fuck ★★	61

5.7

Admission Crack	36
Bad Badille	61
Box, The	17
CMC Route	73
Emergency Entrance	36
I.V. League	36
Initial Route ★	9, 10
Joy	8
Nomad's Land	68
Northwest Ridge, Mt. Thorodin	73
Plague Boys	35
Pooh Belly	9
Remission ★★	36
Sego Conspiracy	26
Serendipity ★	53
Southwest Face, Piz Badille (R)	61
Twin Cracks Variation	75
Unknown, Mushroom Massif	26
Unnamed, Mushroom Massif	27
Wimpy I (R)	79

5.8

Beamer Up, Scotty	9
Blow Chow	44, 45
Civic Minded ★	9
Crescent Moon	79
Dihedral	17
Ellis-Galbraith Route (R)	73, 74
Great Escapade, The (R)	61
Higher Spire ★	44, 45
Mushroom, The ★★	26
99% Pure	38, 39
Original Route, Observatory Rock ★	38, 39
Pollemor ★	26
Roadside Rock, Left Side ★	31
Shake 'n' Bake	53
Sirocco	73
Twin Cracks	75
Unknown Slab Route, Left Infirmary Slab (R)	37
Unnamed, Mushroom Massif	27
Unnamed, Mushroom Massif	27
West Face Route, Ralston Roost	69

5.8+

Casual Corner	51
Dipshit Boss (R)	37
Great Tree Route ★	29
Hidden Pleasures	55
I Spy (R)	30
Lick My Plate ★	53
Vrain Dead	43
Wax 'n' Wane (R)	37

5.9—

Energon Cube	9
Cellulite War	27
Crack, Monkey Skull	51
Dire Spire	44, 45
Roundabout	30
Tapestry	30
Too Many Puppies ★★	61
Watchtower Corner ★	58

5.9

Alvino's Variation	51
Bangyerded	69
Climb to Safety	41
Coldwater Drama	26
End of the Line	79
Explorer Scout	72
Fever Dance Variation ★	51
For Love of Mothernot	73
Forgotten Passage ★	40
Gorilla's Delimna	73
I'm Camming, I'm Camming	29

North Face Variation,
  Desdomona ★ 28
Percepter 79
Rubble Ramble (R) 73
Short Takes 29
Spy Story 30
Vrain Storm (R/X) 53

5.9+
Acts of Contrition 35
Crooked Cross ★★★ 30
Escape from Zonerland 61
Grimlock 79
Outland 73
Papal Bull 73
Pooh Corner 17
Reusable Love Bag ★★ 61
Son of Purina 68
Streatch 53
Unknown, Mushroom Massif (R) 27
Unknown, Piz Badille 61
Unknown, Roadside Rock ★ 31

5.10a
Alley Cat Street ★★★ 41
Brewski 69
Buick, The ★ 9
Central West Face (R) 46
Frenzy 79
Green Slab ★★ 8, 9
Kiss Face 9
Knuckle Sandwich 79
Longhaired Freaky People 79
Mr. Misty 73
Panic in the Gray Room ★★★ 36

Pilly the Pimp 69
Southern Cross ★ 30
Summit Block, Monkey Skull 51
Tigers in Lipstick ★ 18
Unnamed, December Wall 29
Violator, The 57
Wookie ★ 27

5.10b
Caesar's Crack ★ 29
Choir Boys, The 73
Dog Will Hunt 53
I Promise Not To
  Cam In Your Mouth 29
Man Bites Dog ★ 33

North Arête, Bullshit Rock 46
North Corner,
  Wailing Wall ★ 44, 47
Pope on a Rope (R) 73
Ranklands of Infinity ★ 29
Skin Mechanic ★ 38, 39
Southside Corner, Ralston Roost 69
Sunshine Dihedral ★★★ 51
Unknown, Son of Ralston 68
Unnamed, December Wall 29
Unnamed, River Wall (TR) 17
Upside The Cranium ★★★★ 51
White Line Fever 41

5.10c
Amy, Good Gorilla 51
Fever Dance ★★ 51
Fringe Dweller ★★ 51
Full Nelson Reilly ★★ 44, 45
Independent Worm Saloon ★★ 32
Tain't No Crack ★★ 11
Three Stigmata, The 44, 47
Warm Up Climb ★★ 56
Winter Dreams aka Gene and
  George's Excellent Adventure ★★ 29

5.10d
Giveaway, The ★ 48, 49
Introducing Meteor Dad ★★★ 17
Live Wire ★★ 17
Mercy Slab 14
Narrows Crack ★ 41
North Face, Desdomona ★★ 28
Pondemonium ★★★ 53
Shades of Murky Depths 13, 17
Spy Dust ★★ 19
Unknown Face, Buick Rocks ★★ 9

5.11a
Acrophilia ★★ 54
Blaster 79
Bullshit Detector 44, 46
Earthbound Misfit 78
Glass Bead Game, The ★★ 38, 39
Gumby Parade ★★ 55
Hairway To Steven ★★ 33
Hollow Be Thy Name ★★ 51
Nocturnal Leg Muscle Cramp 79
Pontiac ★ 9
Rain Fuck 69
Unnamed, Mushroom Massif 27

Veedub   9
Vrain Child ★   43
Where Eagles Die   19

5.11b
Acrophilia Direct   54
Business Loop ★★   58
Cling to Safety ★★   41
Gene's Route (R)   69
Gravity's Rainbow ★★★   32
Pope on Dope   73
Shuffling Madness ★★★   25
Trojan Crack   63
Unknown, Little Ogre   49
Weight of the World ★★   25

5.11c
Escape From Alcatraz ★★★   17
Hardman Jr.   79
Hitler's Sex Life   10
Infamous Pink Thunderbird ★   9
Ogre Corner ★★★   48, 49
Top Rope, Hitler's Sex Life   9, 10
Trespassers Will Be Violated   57
Turning Point, The ★   56
Via Dolorosa (A0)   63
Zebra Crack aka Glitter Leopard   78

5.11d
Alex in Wonderland   63
Crack Therapy ★★   56
Fat Girls on Mopeds (R)   9
Gestapo Mega (R)   9, 10
Le Diamant E'ternal Direct (R)   17
Open to Suggestions   14
Pocket Hercules ★★★   15, 17
Stressor, The   14
Wages of Sin, The ★★★   47

5.12a
Big, Big Gunky Man (R) ★   15, 17
Cure, The   36
Death Tongue   41
Death Tongue Variation ★★★   41
Flash Flood ★   41
Flying Saucers   63
Highway Robbery ★★★   58
Neurosurgeon ★★★   17
Pica   79
Pipeline, The (R)   12
Pretty Blue Gun ★★   19

Red Neck Hero (R)
    ★★★★   13, 15, 17
Stone Knives ★★   26
Unnamed, Old Stage Wall (TR)   63
Widespread Panic ★★★   48, 49

5.12b
Belligerent Buttress ★★★   56
Big, Big Monkey Man ★★★   15, 17
Finger Tattoo   19
Hitcher, The ★   41
Pon Scum ★   42
Sharps 50 ★★★   19
Wilford Roof   38

5.12c
Dragon Lady   63
Gold Jugular Vein ★★★   56
Jugular Vein ★★   56
Nuttin' but Button ★★★   14
Bambi ★★★   14
Killer Instinct ★★★   38, 39
New Horizon ★★★★   15
Perfect Stemetry ★★   56
Unknown, Observatory Rock   39

5.13
Don't Blame the Youth   79
Open Project   31, 33

5.13a
Old Yellar ★★★   13, 14
Solstice, The   63

5.13b
Brother From
    Another Planet ★★★★   15, 17
Bullfight ★★   42
Gold Finger ★★★   56
Le Diamant E'ternal ★★★★   17
Witch Doctor ★   56

5.13c
Gold Stiletto ★★★★   56

5.13d
Stiletto ★★★★   56

5.14
Lost Horizon ★★   15

ROUTE NAME INDEX

Formations and areas are in capital letters.

A

ACROPHILE ROCK   54
Acrophilia (11a) ★★   54
Acrophilia Direct (11b)   54
Acts of Contrition (9+)   35
Admission Crack (7)   36
Alex in Wonderland (11d)   63
Alley Cat Street (10a) ★★★   41
Alvino's Variation (9)   51
Amy, Good Gorilla (10c)   51
AQUEDUCT ROCK   12

B

Bad Badille (7)   61
Bambi (12d) ★★★   14
Bangyerded (9)   69
Beamer Up, Scotty (8)   9
Belligerent Buttress (12b) ★★★   56
Biege Spider (6)   74
Big, Big Gunky Man
   (12a R) ★   15, 17
Blaster (11a)   79
Blow Chow (8)   44, 45
BOULDERING WALL,
   Buttonrock Dam   20
Box, The (7)   17
Brewski (10a)   69
Brother From
   Another Planet (13b) ★★★★   15, 17
Buick, The (10a) ★   9
BUICK ROCKS   8
   First Buttress   8
   Second Buttress   9
THE BULLET   19
Bullfight (13b) ★★   42
Bullshit Detector (11a)   44, 46
BULLSHIT ROCK   44, 46
Business Loop (11b) ★★   58

C

Caesar's Crack (10b) ★   29
Casual Corner (8+)   51
Cellulite War (9-)   27
Central West Face (10a R)   46
Choir Boys, The (10b)   73

Civic Minded (8) ★   9
Climb to Safety (9)   41
Cling to Safety (11b) ★★   41
CLINICAL PINNACLE   36
CMC Route (7)   73
Coldwater Drama (9)   26
Crack (9-)   51
Crack Therapy (11d) ★★   56
Crescent Moon (8)   79
Crooked Cross (9+) ★★★   30
Cure, The (12a)   36

D

Death Tongue (12a)   41
Death Tongue
   Variation (12a) ★★★   41
DECEMBER WALL   29
Descent Route,
   Mt. Thorodin (2 X)   73, 74
DESDOMONA   28
Dihedral (8)   17
Dipshit Boss (8+ R)   37
Dire Spire (9-)   44, 45
Dog Will Hunt (10b)   53
Don't Blame the Youth (13)   79
Dragon Lady (12c   63

E

Earthbound Misfit (11a)   78
Ellis-Galbraith Route (8 R)   73, 74
Emergency Entrance (7)   36
End of the Line (9)   79
Energon Cube (9-)   9
ENTRYWAY SLABS   8
Escape From Alcatraz (11c) ★★★   17
Escape from Zonerland (9+)   61
Explorer Scout (9)   72

F

THE FANG   56
Fat Girls on Mopeds (11d R)   9
Fever Dance (10c) ★★   51
Fever Dance Variation (9) ★   51
Finger Tattoo (12b)   19
First Door (6)   8
Flash Flood (12a) ★   41

Flying Saucers (12a) 63
For Love of Mothernot (9) 73
Forgotten Passage (9) ★ 40
Frenzy (10a) 79
Fringe Dweller (10c) ★★ 51
Full Nelson Reilly (10c) ★★ 44, 45

G

GUARDIAN ROCK 25
Gene's Route (11b R) 69
Gestapo Mega (11d R) 9, 10
Giveaway, The (10d) ★ 48, 49
Glass Bead Game (11a) ★★ 38, 39
Gold Finger (13b) ★★★ 56
Gold Jugular Vein (12c) ★★★ 56
Gold Stiletto (13c) ★★★★ 56
Goldilocks (6) 79
Gorilla's Delimna (9) 73
Gravity's Rainbow (11b) ★★★ 32
Great Escapade, The (8 R) 61
Great Tree Route (8+) ★ 29
Green Slab (10a) ★★ 8, 9
Grimlock (9+) 79
Gumby Parade (11a) ★★ 55

H

Hairway To Steven (11a) ★★ 33
Hardman Jr. (11c) 79
Hidden Pleasures (8+) 55
HIDEAWAY DOME 55
Higher Spire (8) ★ 44, 45
Highway Robbery (12a) ★★★ 58
Hitcher, The (12b) ★ 41
HITLER'S SEX LIFE 9
Hitler's Sex Life (11c) 10
Hollow Be Thy Name (11a) ★★ 51

I

I Promise Not To Cam
    In Your Mouth (10b) 29
I Spy (8+ R) 30
I.V. League (7) 36
I'm Camming, I'm Camming (9) 29
Independent
    Worm Saloon (10c) ★★ 32
Infamous Pink
    Thunderbird, The (11c) ★ 9
INFIRMARY SLAB 34
    Left 37
    Lower Infirmary 35
    Upper Infirmary 36
Initial Route (7) ★ 9, 10

Introducing Meteor
    Dad (10d) ★★★ 17

J

Joy (7) 8
Jugular Vein (12c) ★★ 56

K

Killer Instinct (12d) ★★★ 38, 39
Kiss Face (10a) 9
Knuckle Sandwich (10a) 79

L

Le Diamant E'ternal (13b) ★★★★ 17
Le Diamant E'ternal
    Direct (11d R) 17
LEATHERFACE 53
Lick My Plate (8+) ★ 53
LITTLE OGRE 48, 49
    North Side 48
Live Wire (10d) ★★ 17
Longhaired Freaky People (10a) 79
Lost Horizon (14a) ★★ 15

M

Man Bites Dog (10b) ★ 33
Mercy Slab (10d) 14
Mr. Misty (10a) 73
MONKEY SKULL 50
Morning Oyster (6) 35
MOUNT THORODIN 71
    First Buttress 75
    Second Buttress 73
    Third Buttress 72
Mushroom, The (8) ★★ 26
MUSHROOM MASSIF 26

N

Narrows Crack (10d) ★ 41
NARROWS SLABS 41
    North 41
    South 42
Neurosurgeon (12a) ★★★ 17
New Horizon (12d) ★★★★ 15
99% Pure (8) 38, 39
Nocturnal Leg
    Muscle Cramp (11a) 79
Nomad's Land (7) 68
North Arête, Bullshit Rock (10b) 46
North Corner,
    Wailing Wall (10b) ★ 44, 47

North Face,

    Desdomona (10d) ★★   28

North Face Variation,

    Desdomona (9) ★   28

Northwest Ridge,

    Mt. Thorodin (7)   73

Nuttin' but Button (12c) ★★★   14

O

OBSERVATORY ROCK   38

  SOUTH SIDE   39

Ogre Corner (11c) ★★★   48, 49

OLD STAGE WALL   63

Old Yellar (13a) ★★★   13, 14

OLD YELLAR FORMATION   13

Open Project (13)   31, 33

Open to Suggestions (11d)   14

Original Route,

    Observatory Rock (8) ★   38, 39

Outland (9+)   73

P

Padding About (5)   75

Panic in the

    Gray Room (10a) ★★★   36

Papal Bull (9+)   73

Percepter (9)   79

Perfect Stemetry (12d) ★★   56

Pica (12a)   79

Pilly the Pimp (10a)   69

PINECLIFFE   77, 78

Pipeline, The (12a R)   12

PIZ BADILLE   61

Plague Boys (7)   35

Pocket Hercules (11d) ★★★   15, 17

Pollemor (8) ★   26

Pon Scum (12b) ★   42

Pondemonium (10d) ★★★   53

Pontiac (11a) ★   9

Pooh Belly (7)   9

Pooh Corner (9+)   17

Pope on a Rope (10b R)   73

Pope on Dope (11b)   73

Pretty Blue Gun (12a) ★★   19

R

Rain Fuck (11a)   69

RALSTON ROOST   69

Ranklands of Infinity (10b) ★   29

RAVEN KNOB   73

Red Neck Hero

    (12a R) ★★★★   13, 15, 17

Remission (7) ★★   36

Reusable Love Bag (9+) ★★   61

Rick's Respite (6)   73

Ridge, The (6) ★★   61

RIVER WALL   13

ROADSIDE ROCK   31

Roadside Rock, Left Side (8) ★ 31

ROB'S ROCK   11

Rock Biter (3)   8

Roundabout (9-)   30

Rubble Ramble (9 R)   73

S

SCOUT ROCK   24

Sego Conspiracy (7)   26

THE SENTINEL   30

Serendipity (7) ★   53

Shades of

    Murky Depths (10d)   13, 17

Shake 'n' Bake (8)   53

Sharps 50 (12b) ★★★   19

Short Takes (9)   29

Shuffling Madness (11b) ★★★ 25

Sidetrack (6)   42

Sirocco (8)   73

Skin Mechanic (10b) ★   38, 39

Solstice, The (13a)   63

Son of Purina (9+)   68

SON OF RALSTON   68

Southern Cross (10a) ★   30

Southside Corner,

    Ralston Roost (10b)   69

Southwest Face,

    Piz Badille (7 R)   61

SPIRE ROCK   44, 45

Spy Dust (10d) ★★   19

Spy Story (9)   30

Stiletto (13d) ★★★★   56

Stone Knives (12a) ★★   26

Streatch (9+)   53

Stressor, The (11d)   14

Summit Block,

    Monkey Skull (10a)   51

Sunshine Dihedral (10b) ★★★ 51

SUPERCHUNK   33

SWEAT LOAF   32

Sympathetic Mind Fuck (6) ★★ 61

T

Tain't No Crack (10c) ★★   11

Tapestry (9-)   30

Three Stigmata, The (10c) 44, 47

THORODIN SLAB — 74
Tigers in Lipstick (10a) ★ — 18
TIGERS IN LIPSTICK
   FORMATION — 18
Too Many Puppies (9-) ★★ — 61
Top Rope,
   Hitler's Sex Life (11c) — 9, 10
Trespassers Will
   Be Violated (11c) — 57
TROJAN BUNNY BUTTRESS — 52
   East Face — 52
   West Face — 53
Trojan Crack (11b) — 63
Turning Point, The (11c) ★ — 56
Twin Cracks (8) — 75
Twin Cracks Escape (4) — 75
Twin Cracks Variation (7) — 75
Unknown Face,
   Buick Rocks (10d) ★★ — 9
Unknown, Little Ogre (11b) — 49
Unknown, Mushroom Massif (7) — 26
Unknown,
   Mushroom Massif (9+ R) — 27
Unknown,
   Observatory Rock (12d) — 39
Unknown, Piz Badille (9+) — 61
Unknown, Roadside Rock (9+) ★ — 31
Unknown Slab Route,
   Left Infirmary Slab (8+ R) — 37
Unknown, Son of Ralston (10b) — 68
Unnamed, December Wall (10b) — 29
Unnamed, December Wall (10a) — 29
Unnamed, Mushroom Massif (7) — 27
Unnamed, Mushroom Massif (8) — 27
Unnamed, Mushroom Massif (8) — 27
Unnamed, Mushroom Massif (11a) — 27
Unnamed,
   Old Stage Wall (12a TR) — 63
Unnamed, River Wall (10b TR) — 17
Upside The
   Cranium (10b) ★★★★ — 51

V

Veedub (11a) — 9
Via Dolorosa (11c A0) — 63
Violator, The (10a) — 57
VIOLATOR BUTTRESS — 57
Vrain Child (11a) ★ — 43
Vrain Dead (8+) — 43
VRAIN DEAD FORMATION — 43
Vrain Storm (9 R/X) — 53

W

Wages of Sin, The (11d) ★★★ — 47
WAILING WALL — 44, 47
Warm Up Climb (10c) ★★ — 56
THE WATCHTOWER — 58
Watchtower Corner (9-) ★ — 58
Wax 'n' Wane (8+ R) — 37
Weight of the World (11b) ★★ — 25
West Face Route,
   Ralston Roost (8) — 69
Where Eagles Die (11a) — 19
White Line Fever (10b) — 41
Widespread Panic (12a) ★★★ — 48, 49
Wilford Roof (12b) — 38
Wimpy I (7 R) — 79
Winter Dreams aka
   Gene and George's
   Excellent Adventure (10c) ★★ — 29
Witch Doctor (13b) ★ — 56
Wookie (10a) ★ — 27

X, Y, Z

YE OLDE ROCK — 40
Zebra Crack aka
   Glitter Leopard (11c) — 78
ZEBRA ROCK — 77, 78

ACCESS: It's every climber's concern

The Access Fund, a national, non-profit climbers organization, works to keep climbing areas open and to conserve the climbing environment. Need help with closures? land acquisition? legal or land management issues? funding for trails and other projects? starting a local climbers' group? CALL US! Climbers can help preserve access by being committed to Leave No Trace (minimum-impact) practices. Here are some simple guidelines:

• **ASPIRE TO "LEAVE NO TRACE"** especially in environmentally sensitive areas like caves. Chalk can be a significant impact on dark and porous rock—don't use it around historic rock art. Pick up litter, and leave trees and plants intact.

• **DISPOSE OF HUMAN WASTE PROPERLY** Use toilets whenever possible. If toilets are not available, dig a "cat hole" at least six inches deep and 200 feet from any water, trails, campsites, or the base of climbs. *Always pack out toilet paper.* On big wall routes, use a "poop tube" and carry waste up and off with you (the old "bag toss" is now illegal in many areas).

• **USE EXISTING TRAILS** Cutting switchbacks causes erosion. When walking off-trail, tread lightly, especially in the desert where cryptogamic soils (usually a dark crust) take thousands of years to form and are easily damaged. Be aware that "rim ecologies" (the clifftop) are often highly sensitive to disturbance.

• **BE DISCRETE WITH FIXED ANCHORS** *Bolts are controversial and are not a convenience* – don't place 'em unless they are *really* necessary. Camouflage all anchors. Remove unsightly slings from rappel stations (better to use steel chain or welded cold shuts). Bolts sometimes can be used proactively to protect fragile resources – consult with your local land manager.

• **RESPECT THE RULES** and speak up when other climbers don't. Expect restrictions in designated wilderness areas, rock art sites, caves, and to protect wildlife, especially nesting birds of prey. *Power drills are illegal in wilderness and all national parks.*

• **PARK AND CAMP IN DESIGNATED AREAS** Some climbing areas require a permit for overnight camping.

• **MAINTAIN A LOW PROFILE** Leave the boom box and day-glo clothing at home—the less climbers are heard and seen, the better.

• **RESPECT PRIVATE PROPERTY** Be courteous to land owners. Don't climb where you're not wanted.

• **JOIN THE ACCESS FUND** To become a member, make a tax-deductible donation of $25.

the ACCESS FUND

The Access Fund
Preserving America's Diverse Climbing Resources
PO Box 17010
Boulder, CO 80308
303.545.6772 • www.accessfund.org